Kamado Smoker and Grill Cookbook for Beginners

600-Day Quick and Easy Recipes for the Most Flavorful and Delicious Barbecue

Leard Mobince

© Copyright 2021 Leard Mobince - All Rights Reserved.

In no way is it legal to reproduce, duplicate, or transmit any part of this document by either electronic means or in printed format. Recording of this publication is strictly prohibited, and any storage of this material is not allowed unless with written permission from the publisher. All rights reserved.

The information provided herein is stated to be truthful and consistent, in that any liability, regarding inattention or otherwise, by any usage or abuse of any policies, processes, or directions contained within is the solitary and complete responsibility of the recipient reader. Under no circumstances will any legal liability or blame be held against the publisher for any reparation, damages, or monetary loss due to the information herein, either directly or indirectly.

Respective authors own all copyrights not held by the publisher.

Legal Notice:

This book is copyright protected. This is only for personal use. You cannot amend, distribute, sell, use, quote or paraphrase any part of the content within this book without the consent of the author or copyright owner. Legal action will be pursued if this is breached.

Disclaimer Notice:

Please note the information contained within this document is for educational and entertainment purposes only. Every attempt has been made to provide accurate, up-to-date and reliable, complete information. No warranties of any kind are expressed or implied. Readers acknowledge that the author is not engaging in the rendering of legal, financial, medical or professional advice.

By reading this document, the reader agrees that under no circumstances are we responsible for any losses, direct or indirect, which are incurred as a result of the use of information contained within this document, including, but not limited to, errors, omissions, or inaccuracies.

Table of Contents

Introduction 6
Chapter 1: Grilling 7

Bacon-Infused Cheeseburgers3 7
Dry-Brined Chicken Breasts With Alabama White Barbecue Sauce 9
Bourbon-Glazed Bone-In Rib-Eye Steak 10
Applewood Bacon-Wrapped Filet Mignon With Tarragon Butter 12
Crispy-Skin Salmon With Chermoula 14
The Perfect Beef Burger 15
Pork Souvlaki 17
Stupid Easy London Broil 18
New York Strip With Summer Tomato And Blue Cheese "Salsa" 19
Shrimp Tostadas 20
Carne Asada 21
Bacon-Wrapped Pork Tenderloin With Rosemary 22
The Perfect Steak....................................23
Hanger Steak With Grilled Onions....24
Serbian Pita Burgers With Roasted Red Pepper Spread 26
Vietnamese Lemongrass Pork 28
Lamb Burgers With Feta, Red Onion, And Tzatziki......................................29
Grilled Pork Noodle Salad 30
Flank Steak With Chimichurri 31
Tandoori Chicken 32

Chapter 2: Smoking 33

Sweet Jewish-Style Brisket...................33
Smoked Boneless Short Ribs with Hoisin Glaze and Kimchi................... 35
Smoked Garlic Beef Tenderloin 36
Barbecue Shrimp Po'boys....................38
Baby Back Ribs 39
Lou's Grilled Meat Loaf....................40
Dry-Rubbed Spareribs...................... 42
Texas-Style Beef Brisket......................43
Carolina Pulled Pork 44
Shortcut Pastrami................................ 45
Memphis Barbecue Pizza....................46
Kansas City Prime Rib 47
Smoke-Barbecued Bologna 49
Beer Can Chicken 50
Pulled Pork Nachos 51
Hugh Lynn's Texas Brisket With An Onion Twist 52
Gilroy Smoked Tri-tip 53
Smoky Slab of Beef Ribs 54
Jerk Chicken 55
Pulled Pork Tacos With Charred Tomatillo Salsa....................................56

Chapter 3: Roasting 57

Classic Roast Chicken 57
Roasted Rack Of Lamb With Thyme .58
Charred Whole Beef Tenderloin With Romesco Sauce 59

Cornish Game Hens With Jalapeño Pesto 61
Cauliflower With Olives And Toasted Bread Crumbs 63
Everyday Roasted Chicken 64
Bok Choy With Soy, Sesame, And Garlic 65
Your Goose Is Cooked 66
Broccoli With Lemon Zest And Parmesan 67
Greek Potato Wedges 68
Marinated Herb-Mustard Leg of Lamb 69
Sunday-Best Pork Loin Roast With Thyme-Fig Balsamic Marinade 71
Steakhouse Roast 73
Moroccan Roasted Carrots 74
Roasted Pork Loin Stuffed With Bacon-Onion Jam, Mascarpone, Apricots, And Plums 75
Pollo A La Brasa 77
Baku Eggplant Salad 78
Cuban Roast Pork (Pernil) 79
Roasted Side Of Salmon With Herb Goat Cheese And Spinach 80
Papas Con Rajas 81

Chapter 4: Steaming & Braising 82

New England Shore Dinner Without The Shore 82
Steamed Tilefish With Orange, Ginger, And Green Onions 84
Kamado Brunswick Stew 85
Italian-Style Braised Rabbit 87
Pork Osso Buco 89
Mussels With Shallots, Tomatoes, And Basil 91
Braised Leeks In Parmesan Cream 93
Chicago-Style Italian Beef Sandwiches 94
Red Wine-Braised Short Ribs 95
Orange-Braised Endive With Kalamata Olives 97
Aloo Gobi 98
Braised Lamb Shanks 100
Classic Beef Stew 102
Grill-Braised Coq Au Vin 104
Frogmore Stew For A Party 106
Tuscan-Style White Beans 107
Kashmiri Braised Lamb (Rogan Josh) 108
Burgoo 110
Coq Au Vin 111
Lobio 113

Chapter 5: Baking 114

Kamado S'Mores 114
Sweet Potato Biscuits with Orange-Honey Butter 115
Proper Cornbread 117
Country Sausage-Laced Baked Beans .118
Sweet Potato Pie 119
Cornbread 120
Molasses Cake 121
Savory Baked Apples 122
Pumpkin Pie 123
Oatmeal-Berry Crisp 124
Meatballs In Tomato Sauce 126
Twice-Baked Potatoes 127
Jerk-Marinated Tofu 129

Shakshouka 130
Mediterranean Baked Fish 131
Dirty Rice 132
Biscuit Breakfast Pudding 134
Pancetta Frittata 136
BEC PizZa............................. 137
Molasses Baked Beans.................. 138

Chapter 6: Rubs, Sauces and more 140

Middle Eastern Za'tar Seasoning 140
Tandoori Seasoning................... 141
Aioli 142
Lemon-Herb Marinade 143
Jerk Marinade 144
Nikki's Lamb Marinade................ 145
Memphis-Style Dry Rub 146
Cajun Rub 147
Limeade Pacific Seafood Marinade .. 148
Japanese Shichimi 149
Kansas City-Style Barbecue Sauce..... 150
Peruvian Cilantro Sauce.............. 151
Canadian-Style Steak Seasoning....... 152
Best Ever Barbecue Rub 153
Tomato Sauce 154
Texas Brisket Rub.................... 155
Alabama White Barbecue Sauce 156
Mojo Marinade 157
Chimichurri.......................... 158
Roasted Red Pepper Spread............ 159

Conclusion 160

Introduction

Kamado Smoker and Grill Cookbook contains all the tips, tricks, and recipes you need to become the master of this versatile backyard grill. Great for new and experienced grillers alike, this definitive kamado grill cookbook teaches everything from first firing up your kamado to using its unique heating properties for the most efficient cooking possible. Learn to grill, smoke, roast, and bake professionally with a variety of mouthwatering recipes—including classic favorites.

Discover the power of the Kamado Smoker and Grill, and learn how you can turn this versatile indoor grilling machine into your go-to kitchen appliance. Whether you've just unboxed yours or you're looking for new ways to make the most of it, this grilling cookbook will give you everything you need to serve mouth-watering meals.

Chapter 1: Grilling

Bacon-Infused Cheeseburgers3

Serves 6

Ingredients:

- 1 pound 80% lean ground chuck
- 1/2 pound 90% lean ground sirloin
- 1/2 pound sliced bacon, cooked to 80% done (don't let it get crispy), drained on paper towels, and finely chopped
- Kosher salt and freshly ground black pepper
- 3 tablespoons unsalted butter, at room temperature
- 6 hamburger buns
- 6 slices Swiss cheese
- 1 ripe avocado, peeled, pitted, thinly sliced, and sprinkled with a little lemon juice
- Lettuce, tomato, onion, and condiments of your choice for serving

Method:

1. Using a light hand, work the meats and bacon together gently. Divide into 6 equal portions and carefully form into six 1-inch-thick patties. Take your thumb and make a good 1/4-inch depression in the middle of each patty; this will keep them from puffing up on the grill. Sprinkle the patties on both sides with salt and pepper. Butter the cut sides of the buns.
2. Light a fire in the kamado grill using your favorite method. After about 10 minutes, place the grill rack in position, close the dome, and open the upper and lower dampers all the way. When the temperature reaches 600°F, adjust the dampers to maintain the temperature. Remember, even when grilling, the dome should be closed as much as possible.
3. Place the burgers on the grill and close the dome. Cook 4 to 6 minutes and flip over. Place the cheese on the burgers, close the dome, and cook another 4 to 5 minutes for medium; add a few more minutes for medium well. The burger's

internal temperature should be between 140 and 160°F. About a minute or two before the burgers are done, place the buns on the grill, cut side down, to toast.
4. Transfer the burgers to a warm platter. Keep the buns on a separate platter. Let your diners construct their own burgers with the fixings and condiments.

Dry-Brined Chicken Breasts With Alabama White Barbecue Sauce

Serves 4

Ingredients:

- 4 (8-ounce) boneless, skinless chicken breasts kosher salt
- Vegetable oil, for coating the chicken
- 1/2 cup alabama white barbecue sauce

Method:

1. Season the chicken generously with salt. Refrigerate overnight.
2. Pat the chicken dry.
3. Prepare the grill for direct grilling at 500°F.
4. Lightly coat the chicken with oil.
5. Put the chicken on the grate. Close the lid and cook, flipping halfway through, for 10 to 12 minutes total or until an instant-read thermometer inserted into the thickest point registers 165°F. Serve immediately with the sauce.

Bourbon-Glazed Bone-In Rib-Eye Steak

Serves 4

Ingredients:

- 4 bone-in rib-eye steaks, 1½ inches thick (about 10 ounces each)
- Canadian-Style Steak Seasoning or kosher salt and freshly ground black pepper
- Olive oil
- 1/4 cup (1/2 stick) unsalted butter
- 1/4 cup diced red onion
- 1/2 cup dark steak sauce, like A-1
- 2 to 4 tablespoons bourbon
- 1 tablespoon molasses
- 2 teaspoons yellow mustard

Method:

1. At least 30 minutes before you plan to grill, remove the steaks from the refrigerator. Generously season both sides and brush with oil.
2. In a small saucepan over medium heat, melt the butter. Add the onion and cook, stirring a few times, until it wilts or, as a friend of mine says, "gets lazy," about 3 minutes. Add the steak sauce, bourbon, molasses, and mustard and stir to combine. Bring to a simmer and cook for 3 to 5 minutes. Remove from the heat. This sauce can be made up to a couple of days in advance and refrigerated. (Let it come to room temperature or gently reheat before using it.)
3. Light a fire in the kamado grill using your favorite method. After about 10 minutes, place the grill rack in position, close the dome, and open the upper and lower dampers all the way. When the temperature reaches between 500 and 600°F, adjust the dampers to maintain the temperature in that range. Remember, even when grilling, the dome should be closed as much as possible.
4. Place the steaks on the grill, close the dome, and cook for about 3 minutes. Rotate the steaks 90 degrees and cook for another 3 minutes. Flip the steaks and cook until well marked and cooked to your liking, about another 5 minutes for medium

rare. During the last couple minutes of cooking, brush the steaks on both sides with the sauce and let it form a glaze.
5. Transfer the steaks to a warm platter and let rest for 5 to 10 minutes. Serve with the remaining bourbon steak glaze passed at the table.

Applewood Bacon-Wrapped Filet Mignon With Tarragon Butter

Serves 4

Ingredients:

- 1/2 cup (1 stick) unsalted butter, softened
- 2 tablespoons chopped fresh tarragon
- 1/2 teaspoon tarragon vinegar
- Kosher salt and freshly ground black pepper
- 8 slices thick-cut applewood-smoked bacon
- 4 filets mignon, 1½ inches thick (about 10 ounces each)
- Kitchen twine
- Canadian-Style Steak Seasoning
- Olive oil for brushing

Method:

1. At least 2 hours before you plan to grill, combine the butter, tarragon, vinegar, and a sprinkling of salt and pepper in a small bowl, using a fork to mash everything together thoroughly. This compound butter will keep, in an airtight container, in the refrigerator for up to a week and up to 3 months in the freezer.
2. Bring a saucepan half full of water to a boil over high heat. Add the bacon, reduce the heat to medium, and blanch for about 5 minutes. Remove using tongs or a slotted spoon and transfer the bacon to paper towels to drain and dry out a bit.
3. At least 30 minutes before you plan to grill, remove the filets from the refrigerator and wrap each with 2 slices of bacon, securing them in place with kitchen twine. Season both sides of the steak generously with steak seasoning, then brush both sides with olive oil.
4. Light a fire in the kamado grill using your favorite method. After about 10 minutes, place the grill rack in position, close the dome, and open the upper and lower dampers all the way. When the temperature reaches between 500 and 600°F, adjust the dampers to maintain the temperature in that range. Remember, even when grilling, the dome should be closed as much as possible.

5. Place the filets on the grill, close the dome, and cook for about 4 minutes. Rotate the steaks 90 degrees and cook for another 2 minutes. Flip the filets and cook for another 6 minutes. Your bacon should be getting crisp at this point and the filets should be medium rare. Filets are always best when served medium rare.
6. Transfer the filets to a platter, place a knob of the tarragon butter on each, and let rest for 5 to 10 minutes before serving.

Crispy-Skin Salmon With Chermoula

Serves 4

Ingredients:

- 4 (3- to 4-ounce) skin-on salmon fillets kosher salt
- Vegetable oil, for coating the fillets
- 1/4 cup chermoula

Method:

1. Prepare the grill for direct grilling at 600°F.
2. Pat the salmon dry. Season with salt. Lightly coat with oil.
3. Place the salmon skin-side down on the grate. Close the lid and cook for 1 to 2 minutes or until char marks appear and the skin is crisp.
4. Flip, close the lid, and cook the other side for 30 seconds to 1 minute (the center should remain slightly pink). Serve immediately with the chermoula.

The Perfect Beef Burger

Serves 6

Ingredients:

- 1½ pounds 80% lean ground chuck
- 8 ounces 90% lean ground sirloin
- Kosher salt and freshly ground black pepper
- 3 tablespoons unsalted butter, at room temperature
- 6 good-quality hamburger buns
- 6 slices of your favorite cheese
- 6 slices of dead-ripe tomato
- 6 romaine lettuce leaves
- 6 thin onion slices
- Condiments of your choice

Method:

1. Put the meats in a medium bowl and season with salt and pepper. Don't go crazy with salt, because you're going to add more later. With a very light hand, work the meats and seasonings together. Form into patties that are least 1 inch thick and slightly wider than the buns you intend to use, about a third of a pound of meat per patty. Take your thumb and make a good depression about 1/4 inch deep in the middle of each patty; this will keep them from puffing up on the grill. Season again with salt and pepper. Slather some butter on the cut sides of your buns.
2. Light a fire in the kamado grill using your favorite method. After about 10 minutes, place the grill rack in position, close the dome, and open the upper and lower dampers all the way. When the temperature reaches 600°F, adjust the dampers to maintain the temperature. Remember, even when grilling, the dome should be closed as much as possible.
3. Place the burgers on the grill and close the dome. Cook 4 to 6 minutes, then turn the burgers, close the dome, and cook for another 4 minutes, which will result in a medium pink doneness. If you want a more well done burger, cook about 8 minutes per side. If you want to check doneness using an instant-read

thermometer, insert it through the side of the patty, not through the top; be sure never to cook a burger to an internal temperature of more than 160°F.

4. If you're using cheese, place the cheese on the patties 1 or 2 minutes after you've turned them. During the last minute of cooking time, set the buns on the grill, cut side down, and grill until lightly toasted.

5. Transfer the burgers to a warm platter. Keep the buns on a separate platter. Let your diners construct their own burgers with the fixings and condiments.

Pork Souvlaki

Serves 4

Ingredients:

- 1/2 cup greek yogurt
- 1 teaspoon olive oil
- 1 tablespoon kosher salt
- 1 tablespoon dried oregano
- Juice of 1/2 lemon
- 1½ pounds boneless pork loin, cut into 1-inch dice

Method:

1. In a large bowl, stir together the yogurt, oil, salt, oregano, and lemon juice.
2. Add the pork; toss to coat thoroughly. Refrigerate overnight.
3. Prepare the grill for direct grilling at 500°F. If using wooden skewers, soak them in water for 30 minutes.
4. Shake off any excess marinade, and thread the pork onto the skewers.
5. Put the skewers on the grate. Close the lid and cook, turning halfway, for 6 to 8 minutes total or until grill marks appear and the pork is just cooked through. Serve immediately.

Stupid Easy London Broil

Serves 4 to 6

Ingredients:

- 1 (3- to 3½-pound) flank steak or thick sirloin tip
- 2 cups Italian salad dressing (homemade is great but store-bought is fine)
- 2 tablespoons dry sherry
- 2 teaspoons Worcestershire sauce
- 1 Granny Smith apple, cored, peeled, and thinly sliced

Method:

1. Cut shallow diagonal slits into one side of the steak. This helps it absorb the marinade better. Combine the dressing, sherry, Worcestershire, and apple slices in a 1-gallon zip-top plastic bag. Add the beef, close the bag, and squish the marinade around the meat. Marinate in the refrigerator for at least 24 hours, but 3 days is optimal.
2. Light a fire in the kamado grill using your favorite method. After about 10 minutes, place the grill rack in position, close the dome, and open the upper and lower dampers all the way. When the temperature reaches 600°F, adjust the dampers to maintain the temperature. Remember, even when grilling, the dome should be closed as much as possible.
3. Remove the meat from the bag; discard the marinade and apples. Pat the meat completely dry with paper towels. Place the steak on the grill, close the dome, and cook for about 8 minutes per side or until the steak gives slightly to the touch and the internal temperature is 140°F for medium doneness, which is best for this tougher cut of meat. Transfer to a warm platter and let rest for 5 to 10 minutes. Slice very thinly across the grain and serve.

New York Strip With Summer Tomato And Blue Cheese "Salsa"

Serves 6

Ingredients:

- 6 New York strip steaks, 1½ inches thick (8 to 10 ounces each)
- Kosher salt and freshly ground black pepper (or substitute Canadian-Style Steak Seasoning, page 234)
- Olive oil
- 2 cups sliced cherry tomatoes or chopped regular tomatoes
- 1/2 cup sliced red onion
- 1/4 cup crumbled blue cheese
- 1/4 cup garlic-flavored olive oil
- 2 tablespoons fig-infused balsamic vinegar
- 2 tablespoons finely chopped fresh basil
- A sprinkling of sea salt

Method:

1. At least 30 minutes before you plan to grill, remove the steaks from the refrigerator. Generously salt and pepper both sides and brush with oil.
2. In a medium bowl, combine the remaining ingredients and toss to mix. Let sit at room temperature until the steaks are ready.
3. Light a fire in the kamado grill using your favorite method. After about 10 minutes, place the grill rack in position, close the dome, and open the upper and lower dampers all the way. When the temperature reaches between 500 and 600°F, adjust the dampers to maintain the temperature in that range. Remember, even when grilling, the dome should be closed as much as possible.
4. Place the steaks on the grill, close the dome, and cook 2 to 3 minutes. Rotate the steaks 90 degrees. Cook for another 2 minutes. Flip the steaks and cook until well marked and cooked to your liking, about another 5 minutes for medium rare.
5. Remove the steaks to a warm platter and let rest 5 to 10 minutes before serving. Spoon the "salsa" over the steaks and serve.

Shrimp Tostadas

Serves 4

Ingredients:

- 1 pound 16/20 shrimp, peeled and deveined
- 1 teaspoon vegetable oil
- 1 teaspoon sweet paprika
- 1 teaspoon ground cumin
- 1/4 teaspoon cayenne pepper
- Kosher salt
- 4 corn tortillas
- 1/2 cup charred tomatillo salsa
- 1 medium tomato, finely diced
- Finely diced red onion, for serving
- Chopped fresh cilantro, for serving
- 1 avocado, peeled, pitted, and sliced

Method:

1. Pat the shrimp dry. In a large bowl, toss the shrimp with the oil, paprika, cumin, and cayenne. Season with salt.
2. Prepare the grill for direct grilling at 425°F.
3. Put the shrimp and tortillas on the grate. Close the lid and cook for 4 to 5 minutes or until the shrimp are opaque and the tortillas are crisp.
4. Divide the shrimp among the tostadas. Top with the salsa, tomato, onion, cilantro, and avocado. Serve immediately.

Carne Asada

Serves 4

Ingredients:

- 1 tablespoon chipotle chile powder
- 2 teaspoons hot paprika
- 1 teaspoon ground cumin
- 1 teaspoon dried oregano
- 1/2 teaspoon kosher salt
- 1/8 teaspoon cayenne pepper
- 2 cloves garlic, finely chopped
- 1/4 cup olive oil
- 2 tablespoons fresh lime juice (about 1 lime)
- 1½ pounds skirt steak
- Taco or fajita fixings as desired

Method:

1. Combine the chipotle powder, paprika, cumin, oregano, salt, cayenne, and garlic. Stir in the olive oil and lime juice. Place the skirt steak in a 1-gallon zip-top plastic bag, add the marinade, and squish around to coat the steak well. Seal the bag and let stand at room temperature for at least 30 minutes (an hour is better) and up to 4 hours.
2. Light a fire in the kamado grill using your favorite method. After about 10 minutes, place the grill rack in position, close the dome, and open the upper and lower dampers all the way. When the temperature reaches 500°F, adjust the dampers to maintain the temperature. Remember, even when grilling, the dome should be closed as much as possible.
3. Place the steak on the grill grate, close the dome, and cook for about 4 minutes per side for medium rare or to your desired degree of doneness.
4. Transfer the steak to a cutting board and let rest for about 5 minutes. Thinly slice the steak across the grain and serve as desired.

Bacon-Wrapped Pork Tenderloin With Rosemary

Serves 4 to 6

Ingredients:

- 1 tablespoon finely minced fresh rosemary
- 1/2 teaspoon kosher salt
- 1/2 teaspoon freshly ground black pepper
- 2 pork tenderloins (about 1 pound each)
- 12 slices thinly sliced hickory-smoked bacon (about 3/4 pound)

Method:

1. In a small bowl, combine the rosemary, salt, and pepper. Set aside.
2. Trim the excess fat and silverskin from the tenderloins. Season with the rosemary mixture, rubbing it into the meat. Place 6 slices of the bacon on a cutting board. Place one of the tenderloins in the middle of the bacon slices and wrap the bacon slices around it. Repeat with the second tenderloin and remaining bacon. Let the pork sit at room temperature for about 15 minutes before grilling.
3. Light a fire in the kamado grill using your favorite method. After about 10 minutes, place the grill rack in position, close the dome, and open the upper and lower dampers all the way. When the temperature reaches 500°F, adjust the dampers to maintain the temperature. Remember, even when grilling, the dome should be closed as much as possible.
4. Place the pork on the grill grate, close the dome, and close the dampers halfway. You want to get a fast char, but because of the pork's longer cooking time, the grill temperature should be around 350° to 400°F. Grill the pork, turning it every 15 minutes, until the pork is firm but gives a little to the touch and the internal temperature is 140°F. The temperature will continue to rise while the meat rests.
5. Transfer the pork to a platter and let rest for about 10 minutes. Cut into 2-inch thick slices and serve.

The Perfect Steak

Serves 6

Ingredients:

- 6 T-bone steaks, 1½ inches thick (about 10 ounces each)
- Kosher salt and freshly ground black pepper
- 4 to 6 tablespoons olive oil
- 6 tablespoons (3/4 stick) salted butter, cut into 1-tablespoon pats

Method:

1. At least 30 minutes before you plan to grill, remove the steaks from the refrigerator. Season them generously on both sides with salt and pepper.
2. Light a fire in the kamado grill using your favorite method. After about 10 minutes, place the grill rack in position, close the dome, and open the upper and lower dampers all the way. When the temperature reaches between 600°F and 700°F, adjust the dampers to maintain the temperature in that range. Remember, even when grilling, the dome should be closed as much as possible.
3. Brush the steaks on both sides with the oil. Place the steaks on the grill rack, close the dome, and cook for about 3 minutes. Using tongs or a wide spatula (never a fork, please-you'll lose precious juices through the puncture marks), rotate each steak 90 degrees. This will give you those beautiful crisscross grill marks that will impress your friends and neighbors and add flavor. Cook another 2 to 3 minutes, then flip the steaks. Cook until well marked and done to your liking, another 5 minutes for medium rare (135°F on an instant-read thermometer).
4. Transfer the steaks to a warm platter. Put a pat of butter on each steak and let the steaks rest for 5 to 10 minutes before serving. You should get plenty of oohs and aahs.

Hanger Steak With Grilled Onions

Serves 6

Ingredients:

- 1/4 cup extra-virgin olive oil
- 1/4 cup sherry vinegar or balsamic vinegar
- 1/4 cup tamari
- 2 tablespoons coarse-grain mustard
- 1 tablespoon Dijon mustard
- 1 tablespoon yellow or brown mustard seeds
- 2 teaspoons grated peeled fresh ginger
- 6 cloves garlic, finely minced
- Kosher salt and freshly ground black pepper
- 6 hanger steaks (8 to 10 ounces each)
- 3 large red onions, thickly sliced
- 3 tablespoons balsamic vinegar

Method:

1. In a glass baking dish large enough to hold the steaks in a single layer, whisk the oil, sherry vinegar, tamari, both mustards and mustard seeds, ginger, garlic, and salt and pepper (to taste) together. Add the steaks and turn to coat. Cover with plastic wrap and refrigerate for at least 4 hours and no more than 8 hours, turning them once or twice.
2. About an hour before you plan to grill, remove the steaks from the marinade. Discard the marinade and pat the steaks as dry as possible with a paper towel.
3. Light a fire in the kamado grill using your favorite method. After about 10 minutes, place the grill rack in position, close the dome, and open the upper and lower dampers all the way. When the temperature reaches 600°F, adjust the dampers to maintain the temperature. Remember, even when grilling, the dome should be closed as much as possible.

4. Place the steaks on the grill along with the onion slices, close the dome, and cook for about 5 minutes per side. This cut of meat really should be served medium rare or medium at most (125° to 140°F). Turn the onions when you turn the steaks.

5. When the steaks are done, remove to a warm platter and let rest for 5 to 10 minutes. Meanwhile, slide the onions off the skewers into a medium bowl, separating the rings. Toss with the balsamic vinegar while the onions are still warm. After the steaks have rested, spoon the onions over the steaks and serve.

Serbian Pita Burgers With Roasted Red Pepper Spread

Serves 4

Ingredients:

- 1 tablespoon baking powder
- 1 tablespoon kosher salt
- 2 teaspoons freshly ground black pepper
- 2 teaspoons sweet paprika
- 2 pounds ground lamb
- 6 garlic cloves, grated
- Vegetable oil, for oiling the foil
- 8 pita rounds
- 1/2 cup sour cream
- 1/2 cup roasted red pepper spread
- 1 small red onion, thinly sliced
- 2 medium tomatoes, sliced
- 16 butter lettuce leaves

Method:

1. Prepare the grill for direct grilling at 550°F.
2. In a large bowl, combine the baking powder, salt, pepper, and paprika. Add the lamb and garlic and, using your hands, mix until thoroughly combined.
3. Lightly oil 4 pieces of aluminum foil slightly larger than the size of the pitas. Divide the mixture evenly among them. Form into four 1/4-inch-thick patties, leaving a small border around the edges of the foil.
4. Slide your palm underneath one of the pieces of foil, and quickly turn the patty over onto the grate. Peel the foil off the top of the patty. Repeat with the remaining pieces. Close the lid and cook, flipping halfway through, for 3 minutes total, or until char marks appear. Transfer to plates.
5. Put the pita rounds on the grate. Close the lid and toast for 30 to 60 seconds, or just until grill marks appear. Transfer to a work surface.

6. Spread the sour cream on half the pita rounds and the red pepper spread on the remainder. Place one patty on each red pepper spread pita; layer with onion, tomatoes, and lettuce; and top with the sour cream pitas. Quarter each burger and serve immediately.

Vietnamese Lemongrass Pork

Serves 4

Ingredients:

- 1 (3-inch) piece lemongrass, tough portions discarded, finely chopped
- 3 tablespoons water
- 2 tablespoons fish sauce
- 1 tablespoon light brown sugar
- 4 (4-ounce) boneless center-cut pork chops

Method:

1. In a small saucepan on the stove top, combine the lemongrass, water, fish sauce, and sugar. Heat, stirring, just until it comes to a simmer and the sugar dissolves. Transfer to a shallow heatproof dish.
2. Place the pork between two pieces of plastic wrap; pound to 1/2-inch thickness. Transfer to the dish with the marinade and turn to coat thoroughly.
3. Marinate at room temperature for 1 hour, turning halfway through.
4. Prepare the grill for direct grilling at 650°F.
5. Shake off any excess marinade. Put the pork on the grate. Close the lid and cook, turning once, for 1½ to 2 minutes total or until char marks appear and the pork is just cooked through (it's best with a hint of pink remaining at the center). Serve immediately.

Lamb Burgers With Feta, Red Onion, And Tzatziki

Serves 4

Ingredients:

- 2 pounds ground lamb
- 4 teaspoons kosher salt
- Freshly ground black pepper
- 4 kaiser rolls, split
- 1 cup tzatziki
- Sliced red onion, for topping
- 1/2 cup crumbled feta cheese, for topping

Method:

1. Prepare the grill for direct grilling at 500°F.
2. Meanwhile, in a large bowl, combine the lamb with the salt and pepper. Using your hands, mix until just incorporated; form into four 1-inch-thick patties with a slight dimple in the center.
3. Put the burgers on the grate. Close the lid and cook, flipping halfway through, for 8 to 10 minutes total for medium, or until an instant-read thermometer inserted into the center registers 135°F. (If using store-bought ground lamb, always cook it to 160°F, or well done.) In the last minute of cooking, place the rolls cut-side down on the grate to toast.
4. Spread the tzatziki on the buns and assemble the burgers, topping them with the onion and feta. Serve immediately.

Grilled Pork Noodle Salad

Serves 4

Ingredients:

- 7 ounces dried vermicelli noodles
- 1 recipe vietnamese lemongrass pork, sliced
- 2 cups bean sprouts
- 2 cups fresh cilantro leaves
- 1 cup shredded carrots
- 1 cup shredded daikon or jicama
- 1 cup shredded lettuce
- 1/2 cup vietnamese fish sauce dressing
- 1/2 cup roasted unsalted peanuts, chopped, for garnish

Method:

1. Bring a large saucepan of water to a boil over high heat on the stove top.
2. Add the noodles. Cook according to the package directions. Drain thoroughly.
3. Divide the noodles, pork, bean sprouts, cilantro, carrots, daikon, lettuce, and dressing among four bowls. Toss to coat with the dressing, then top with the peanuts. Serve immediately.

Flank Steak With Chimichurri

Serves 8

Ingredients:

- 1 (2½-pound) flank steak
- Kosher salt
- Vegetable oil, for coating the steak
- Freshly ground black pepper
- 1/2 cup chimichurri

Method:

1. Season the steak generously with salt on both sides. Refrigerate overnight.
2. Pat the steak dry.
3. Prepare the grill for direct grilling at 650°F.
4. Lightly coat the steak with oil.
5. Put on the grate. Close the lid and cook, flipping halfway through, for 6 minutes total for medium, or until an instant-read thermometer inserted into the thickest part registers 135°F.
6. Remove from the heat. Season with pepper. Rest for 10 minutes before slicing thinly across the grain at a 45-degree angle. Serve with the chimichurri on the side.

Tandoori Chicken

Serves 6

Ingredients:

- 4 (8-ounce) boneless, skinless chicken breasts, cut into 1½-to 2-inch chunks
- 1/2 cup greek yogurt
- 2 tablespoons garam masala
- 1 tablespoon kosher salt
- 1 teaspoon vegetable oil
- 1 teaspoon ground coriander
- 1 teaspoon cayenne pepper
- Juice of 1/2 lime

Method:

1. Pat the chicken dry.
2. In a large bowl, stir together the yogurt, garam masala, salt, oil, coriander, cayenne, and lime juice.
3. Add the chicken; toss to coat thoroughly. Refrigerate overnight.
4. Prepare the grill for direct grilling at 500°F. If using wooden skewers, soak in water for 30 minutes.
5. Shake off any excess marinade, and thread the chicken onto the skewers.
6. Put the skewers on the grate. Close the lid and cook for 9 to 10 minutes or until grill marks appear and the chicken is just cooked through. Serve immediately.

Chapter 2: Smoking

Sweet Jewish-Style Brisket

Serves 8 to 10

Ingredients:

- 1/2 cup olive oil
- 1/2 cup cola
- 1/2 cup dry red wine
- 1/4 cup honey
- 5 tablespoons ketchup
- 2 cups finely chopped onions
- 1/2 teaspoon dry mustard, like Colman's
- 1/2 teaspoon smoked paprika
- 1 (5-to 7-pound) beef brisket
- 3 tablespoons unsalted butter or pauvre margarine
- 3 tablespoons gravy flour or all-purpose flour
- Kosher salt and freshly ground black pepper

Method:

1. In a medium bowl, whisk the oil, cola, wine, honey, ketchup, onions, mustard, and paprika together.
2. Place the brisket in a 2½-gallon zip-top plastic bag or other container large enough to hold it. Pour in the marinade and squish everything around. Seal the bag or cover the container and marinate overnight in the refrigerator, turning the bag or brisket over occasionally. About an hour before smoking, remove the brisket from the marinade; reserve the marinade.
3. Light a fire in the kamado grill using your favorite method. After about 10 minutes, close the dome and open the upper and lower dampers all the way. When the temperature reaches 300°F, place the wood chunks around the fire and add any accessories necessary for smoking on your particular grill, along with the

grill rack. Close the dome, let the temperature build back to between 200° and 250°F, and wait for a little smoke to accumulate.

4. Place the brisket on a rack in a drip pan, then place the pan on the grill grate; the pan will catch the drippings, which are good for making sauce or seasoning baked beans. Close the dome and smoke for 5 to 6 hours, until an instant-read thermometer inserted at its thickest point reads 180°F. Remove the brisket from the grill and let cool. When cool, trim off the heavy fat layer, if desired. Wrap the brisket in aluminum foil and refrigerate overnight (trust me, you want to do this; the brisket flavor gets even better). Also refrigerate the brisket drippings and marinade.

5. Preheat the oven to 350°F. reheat the brisket (still wrapped in foil) for about 20 minutes (until heated all the way through). While the brisket reheats, make the gravy, if you like (and I highly recommend that you do). Melt the butter in a small saucepan over medium heat. Add the flour and whisk for 3 to 4 minutes. Very slowly and whisking constantly, add the reserved marinade and drippings from the meat. Cook, stirring, until the gravy thickens to your liking, then taste and season with salt and pepper. Keep warm.

6. Slice the reheated brisket against the grain into thin slices and serve with the gravy poured over.

Smoked Boneless Short Ribs with Hoisin Glaze and Kimchi

Serves 4

Ingredients:

- 2 tablespoons canola oil
- 4 cloves garlic, finely chopped
- 1 (2-inch) piece fresh ginger, peeled and finely chopped
- 1/2 cup hoisin sauce
- 1 tablespoon maple syrup
- Kosher salt and freshly ground black pepper
- 2 pounds boneless short ribs
- Kimchi for serving

Method:

1. Heat the oil in a small saucepan over medium-high heat until it shimmers. Add the garlic and ginger and stir-fry for about 2 minutes. Remove the pan from the heat, stir in the hoisin sauce and maple syrup, and season to taste with salt and pepper. The glaze is ready to use (or you can refrigerate it in an airtight container for 2 to 3 days; let it come to room temperature before using it).
2. Light a fire in the kamado grill using your favorite method. After about 10 minutes, close the dome and open the upper and lower dampers all the way. When the temperature reaches 300°F, place the wood chunks around the fire and add any accessories necessary for smoking on your particular grill, along with the grill rack. Close the dome, let the temperature build back to between 200° and 250°F, and wait for a little smoke to accumulate. Adjust the dampers to maintain the temperature in this range.
3. Place the meat on the grill, close the dome, and smoke for about 45 minutes. At this point, brush the beef with the glaze on both sides, close the dome, and cook until the internal temperature reaches 140°F. Brush again on both sides with glaze, close the dome, and cook another 5 minutes.
4. Transfer the ribs to a platter, brush both sides with the glaze, and serve, passing any remaining glaze at the table along with the kimchi.

Smoked Garlic Beef Tenderloin

Serves 8 to 12

Ingredients:

- 10 cloves garlic
- 1 teaspoon kosher salt
- 1 tablespoon chopped fresh thyme
- 1 tablespoon chopped fresh flat-leaf parsley
- 1 (4-pound) beef tenderloin roast, trimmed of silverskin
- Freshly ground black pepper
- Prepared horseradish sauce

Method:

1. Using the butt of knife, smash each garlic clove on a cutting board and peel it. Sprinkle all the cloves with the salt and, again, using the butt of the knife, mash the garlic into a paste with the salt, working the knife back and forth. Place the garlic paste in a small bowl and work in the herbs. Smear the paste all over the beef, making sure you get the ends as well. Liberally season with black pepper. Place the tenderloin on a wire rack and then place the rack in a disposable aluminum-foil pan to catch the drippings.
2. Light a fire in the kamado grill using your favorite method. After about 10 minutes, close the dome and open the upper and lower dampers all the way. When the temperature reaches 300°F, place the wood chunks around the fire and add any accessories necessary for smoking on your particular grill, along with the grill rack. Close the dome, let the temperature build back to between 200° and 250°F, and wait for a little smoke to accumulate. Adjust the dampers to maintain the temperature in this range.
3. Place the pan on the grill, clos the dome, and smoke the roast for about 2 hours, until the internal temperature in the center reaches 125°F for rare or to your desired degree of doneness.

4. Transfer the roast to a cutting board and let rest for about 30 minutes, tented with foil, if desired. Slice the roast thinly and serve with horseradish sauce on the side and any accumulated pan drippings.

Barbecue Shrimp Po'boys

Serves 4

Ingredients:

- 1 pound 16/20 shrimp, peeled and deveined
- Kosher salt
- Freshly ground black pepper
- 4 tablespoons (1/2 stick) unsalted butter, melted
- 2 tablespoons worcestershire sauce
- 1 teaspoon your favorite hot sauce
- 4 french rolls, split
- 1 cup shredded lettuce
- 1/2 cup chopped tomatoes
- 1/4 cup aioli

Method:

1. Prepare the grill for smoking at 180°F and 200°F
2. Season the shrimp with salt and pepper.
3. Place the shrimp on the grate in a single layer. Close the lid and cook for 25 minutes or just until opaque.
4. In a medium bowl, mix the butter, Worcestershire, and hot sauce; add the shrimp and toss to coat.
5. Divide the shrimp among the four rolls and top with the lettuce, tomatoes, and aioli. Serve immediately.

Baby Back Ribs

Serves 4

Ingredients:

- 4 (2- to 2½-pound) racks baby back ribs
- 3 tablespoons kosher salt
- 3 tablespoons freshly ground black pepper
- 2/3 cup kansas city-style barbecue sauce

Method:

1. Trim any hanging fat off the ribs. Season with the salt and pepper on both sides. Let stand at room temperature for 1 hour.
2. Prepare the grill for smoking at 225°F to 675°F.
3. Place the ribs meat-side up on the grate over the drip pan. Close the lid. If desired, wrap the ribs in aluminum foil after 1 hour 30 minutes or once the bark (crust) is reddish brown.
4. Turn over the ribs, close the lid, and continue cooking for 1 hour 30 minutes more, or until the ribs pull apart with a gentle tug.
5. Remove the foil (if using), baste the ribs with the sauce, close the lid, and cook meat-side up for 10 more minutes or until the sauce is set. Serve immediately.

Lou's Grilled Meat Loaf

Serves 6 to 8

Ingredients:

- 1½ cups seasoned (your choice of flavor) bread crumbs
- 3 tablespoons finely chopped onion
- 2 cloves garlic, minced
- 1/2 teaspoon kosher salt
- 1/2 teaspoon dried oregano
- 1/2 teaspoon dried thyme
- 1/2 teaspoon crushed dried rosemary
- 1/4 teaspoon freshly ground black pepper
- 1/2 cup half-and-half
- 1 pound each ground beef, veal, and pork (or any combination you prefer)
- Your favorite marinara sauce for serving

Method:

1. In a large bowl, combine the bread crumbs, onion, garlic, salt, oregano, thyme, rosemary, and pepper and stir well to combine. Pour in the half-and-half and stir to combine. Add the meat and, using your hands, mix until thoroughly combined.
2. Spray a 9- x 13-inch disposable aluminum-foil pan with cooking spray. Place the meat mixture in the pan and form into a loaf around 3 inches wide and 8 inches long.
3. Light a fire in the kamado grill using your favorite method. After about 10 minutes, close the dome and open the upper and lower dampers all the way. When the temperature reaches 300°F, place the wood chunks around the fire and add accessories necessary for smoking on your particular grill, along with the grill rack. Close the dome, let the temperature build back to between 200° and 250°F, and wait for a little smoke to accumulate. Adjust the dampers to maintain the temperature in this range.

4. Put the pan on the grill, close the dome, and smoke for about 2 hours, until the internal temperature in the center reaches 150° to 160°F. The meat loaf is going to take on a pretty pinkish-brown hue as it smokes.
5. When done, remove from the grill and, using two spatulas, lift the meat loaf from the pan onto a platter. Tent with aluminum foil and let rest a good 30 minutes. Slice and serve with warm marinara sauce.

Dry-Rubbed Spareribs

Serves 6

Ingredients:

- 2 (4-to 5 -pound) racks pork spareribs
- 1/4 cup yellow or whole-grain mustard
- 6 tablespoons memphis-style dry rub

Method:

1. Trim any excess fat from the ribs and square off the edges. Pat dry, then slather with the mustard on both sides. Season with the rub. Let stand at room temperature for 1 hour.
2. Prepare the grill for smoking at 225°F to 675°F.
3. Place the ribs meat-side up on the grate over the drip pan. Close the lid. If desired, wrap in aluminum foil after 3 hours or once the bark (crust) is reddish brown.
4. Turn over the ribs, close the lid, and continue cooking for 2 more hours or until the ribs pull apart with a gentle tug. Serve immediately.

Texas-Style Beef Brisket

Serves 6 to 8

Ingredients:

- 1 (8- to 10-pound) beef brisket
- 3 tablespoons kosher salt
- 3 tablespoons freshly ground black pepper

Method:

1. Trim off any hard fat from the brisket and square off the edges. Trim the fat cap down to an even 1/4-inch thickness. Sprinkle evenly on all sides with the salt and pepper. Refrigerate overnight.
2. Prepare the grill for smoking at 250°F and 275°F.
3. Place the brisket fat-side up on the grate over the drip pan. Close the lid. If desired, wrap in aluminum foil after 5 to 6 hours or once the bark (crust) is dark brown.
4. Turn over the brisket, close the lid, and continue cooking for 2 hours 30 minutes to 3 hours 30 minutes more or until an instant-read thermometer inserted into the center registers 200°F.
5. Rest the brisket, wrapped in foil, for 1 to 2 hours before serving. Cut across the grain into 1/4inch- thick slices. Pour over as much of the drippings from the pan as you like, and serve.

Carolina Pulled Pork

Serves 12

Ingredients:

- 1 (7- to 8-pound) bone-in boston butt
- 2 tablespoons yellow mustard
- 3 tablespoons kosher salt
- 3 tablespoons freshly ground black pepper

Method:

1. Trim the pork of any hard fat, pat dry, and slather with the mustard. Season with the salt and pepper. Refrigerate overnight.
2. Prepare the grill for smoking at 225°F to 275°F.
3. Put the pork on the grate over the drip pan. Close the lid. If desired, wrap the pork in aluminum foil after 7 hours to 7 hours 30 minutes or when an instant-read thermometer inserted into the center without touching the bone registers 160°F.
4. Turn over the pork, close the lid, and continue cooking for 2 hours 30 minutes to 3 hours or until the internal temperature reaches 190°F.
5. Transfer the pork to a large cutting board. When it cools enough that you can comfortably handle it, discard any bones and chop the crispy skin into pieces. Pull the meat into shreds (you can do this with two forks) or chop it. Mix the chopped skin in with the meat when serving.

Shortcut Pastrami

Serves 4 to 6

Ingredients:

- 1 corned beef brisket (4 pounds), low salt preferred, with its spice packet (if there isn't one, use 2 bay leaves and 1/2 teaspoon yellow mustard seeds)
- 1 tablespoon coriander seeds
- 1 tablespoon black peppercorns

Method:

1. Open up the corned beef brisket and cut away any excessive fat. You do want to leave a small fat cap. Pat very dry with paper towels. Grind the contents of the spice packet, the coriander seeds, and peppercorns in a spice grinder or mortar into a coarse mixture. Rub this mixture over all surfaces of the corned beef.
2. Light a fire in the kamado grill using your favorite method. After about 10 minutes, close the dome and open the upper and lower dampers all the way. When the temperature reaches 300°F, add any accessories necessary for smoking on your particular grill, along with the grill rack. Close the dome, let the temperature build back to between 200° and 250°F, and wait for a little smoke to accumulate. Adjust the dampers to maintain the temperature in this range.
3. Place the corned beef on the grill, close the dome, and smoke until the brisket registers and internal temperature of 150°F. I try to keep my grill temperature closer to 200°F because I want the brisket to absorb as much smoke as possible. This process usually takes about 2 hours.
4. Transfer the brisket to a disposable aluminum-foil pan and fill with enough water to come up about 1/2 inch. Cover the pan with foil and crimp it tightly. Place the pan back on the grill, close the dome, adjust the dampers so the temperature is between 200° and 250°F, and steam-roast the brisket until it is extremely tender, which will take another 2 to 3 hours. Remove from the grill, uncover, and let rest for about 10 minutes. Slice the pastrami against the grain and serve as you prefer (I would suggest rye bread, spicy mustard, and sauerkraut).

Memphis Barbecue Pizza

Serves 2

Ingredients:

- 1 (11-ounce) can refrigerated thin-crust pizza dough
- 1/4 cup kansas city-style barbecue sauce
- 2 cups shredded gouda cheese
- 1 cup carolina pulled pork
- 1/4 cup thinly sliced red onion

Method:

1. Bring the grill to 650°F with the cooking grate and heat deflector installed, then preheat a pizza stone on the grate with the lid closed.
2. On a lightly floured work surface, roll out the dough to a 12- to 13-inch diameter.
3. Brush the dough with the sauce.
4. Scatter the cheese, pork, and onion on top.
5. Put the pizza on parchment paper on the stone. Close the lid and cook for 1 to 2 minutes or until the crust is golden brown. Remove from the grill and rest for a few minutes before slicing.

Kansas City Prime Rib

Serves 8 to 10

Ingredients:

- 1 bone-in standing rib roast (about 6 pounds), trimmed of excess fat
- 6 large cloves garlic, peeled
- 2 tablespoons fresh rosemary leaves
- 2 tablespoons fresh thyme leaves
- Kosher salt and freshly ground black pepper
- 3 tablespoons coarse-grain Dijon mustard
- 3 tablespoons olive oil
- Prepared horseradish sauce

Method:

1. At least 1 hour before you're ready to begin cooking, remove the roast from the refrigerator. In a food processor or mortar, combine the garlic, rosemary, thyme, and 2 teaspoons each salt and pepper. Pulse to finely mince or crush with a pestle. Add the mustard and pulse or mix to combine. Slowly add the oil with the food processor running or slowly mix in with the pestle until a paste forms. Smear the paste evenly over the entire surface of the roast. For a more intense herb flavor, let the roast sit at room temperature for 2 hours or wrap and refrigerate overnight.
2. Light a fire in the kamado grill using your favorite method. After about 10 minutes, close the dome and open the upper and lower dampers all the way. When the temperature reaches 300°F, place the wood chunks around the fire and add any accessories necessary for smoking on your particular grill, along with the grill rack. Close the dome, let the temperature build back to between 200° and 250°F, and wait for a little smoke to accumulate. Adjust the dampers to maintain the temperature in this range.
3. Place the roast, bone side down, on a rack in a disposable aluminum-foil pan (this pan is going to catch all the delicious meat juices so you can make gravy). Place the pan on the grill, close the dome, and smoke until an instant-read thermometer

registers 130° to 135°F. Make sure to insert the thermometer away from the bone. Usually this takes about 4 hours, but begin to check after 2½ hours.

4. Transfer the roast to a cutting board, tent with foil, and let rest for at least 30 minutes to let the juices settle. If you wish, make a quick pan gravy (see let) out of the drippings. Carve the meat into thin slices and arrange on a warm platter. Serve at once with horseradish sauce and the gravy.

Smoke-Barbecued Bologna

Serves 4 to 6

Ingredients:

- 1 (3-pound) log of bologna
- Your favorite barbecue sauce for serving
- Dill pickle slices for serving
- Cheap white buns for serving

Method:

1. Light a fire in the kamado grill using your favorite method. After about 10 minutes, close the lid and open the upper and lower dampers all the way. When the temperature reaches 300°F, place the wood chunks around the fire. Now add any accessories necessary for smoking on your particular grill, along with the grill rack. Close the dome, let the temperature build back to between 200° and 250°F, and wait for a little smoke to accumulate. Adjust the dampers to maintain the temperature in this range.
2. Place the bologna on the grill, close the dome, and smoke for about 3 hours, until the internal temperature reaches 180°F.
3. Remove the bologna to a cutting board. Peel off the skin and cut into thick slices. Serve with the barbecue sauce, pickles, and buns.

Beer Can Chicken

Serves 4

Ingredients:

- 1 (4- to 5 -pound) chicken
- Kosher salt
- 2 tablespoons vegetable oil
- 1 (12-ounce) can american lager, such as budweiser, half empty

Method:

1. Season the chicken generously with salt. Refrigerate overnight.
2. Pat the chicken dry.
3. Prepare the grill for smoking at 225°F to 600°F.
4. Coat the chicken with the oil. Insert the beer can into the cavity.
5. Place the chicken on the grate over the drip pan, using the beer can as a stand. Close the lid and cook for 3 to 4 hours or until an instant-read thermometer inserted into the thigh without touching the bone registers 160°F.
6. Rest for 10 minutes before serving. Carve off the breasts, thighs, legs, and wings; slice the breasts and serve.

Pulled Pork Nachos

Serves 4

Ingredients:

- 3 cups carolina pulled pork
- 1/3 cup kansas city-style barbecue sauce
- 4 cups tortilla chips
- 1 cup shredded monterey jack cheese
- 1 jalapeño pepper, stemmed and thinly sliced
- 1/3 cup diced white onion
- 1 (15-ounce) can black beans, drained and rinsed

Method:

1. Bring the grill to 350°F with the heat deflector and cooking grate installed.
2. In a medium bowl, toss the pork with the sauce until thoroughly coated.
3. In a 10-inch cast iron skillet, layer the tortilla chips, pork, cheese, jalapeño pepper, onion, and beans.
4. Put the skillet on the grate. Close the grill lid and cook for 5 to 10 minutes or just until the cheese melts. Serve immediately.

Hugh Lynn's Texas Brisket With An Onion Twist

Serves 12, twice

Ingredients:

- 2 (5-to 6-pound) beef friskets
- 12 cloves garlic, thinly sliced
- 2tablespoons Texas Brisket Rub
- 4 large onions, quartered
- Texas Barbecue Joint-Style Sauced for serving

Method:

1. Using a knife, cut small slits into both briskets and slide a slice of garlic into each slit. Sprinkle each brisket with 1 tablespoon of the brisket rub and work it into the meat. Let sit at room temperature until you're ready to cook.
2. Light a fire in the kamado grill using your favorite method. After about 10 minutes, close the dome and open the upper and lower dampers all the way. When the temperature reaches 300°F, place the wood chunks and the onions around the fire and add any accessories necessary for smoking on your particular grill, along whit the grill rack. Close the dome, let the temperature to come back to between 200° and 250°F, and wait for a little smoke to accumulate. Adjust the dampers to maintain the temperature in this range.
3. Place the briskets on a rack in a drip pan, then place the pan on the grill grate; the pan will catch the drippings, which are good for making sauce or seasoning baked beans. Smoke the briskets for 6 to 8 hours. After 6 hours, check the meat at its thickest point with an instant-read thermometer; 180°F is where you want to be.
4. Remove the briskets from the grill and wrap each in aluminum foil. Let one brisket cool completely, then wrap it again in foil and freeze it; it will keep up to 3 months. (To reheat, let it thaw overnight in the refrigerator, then put it in a preheated 350°F oven until warmed through, about 30 minutes.) Let the other brisket rest for 15 to 20 minutes, then slice thinly across the grain and serve. Pour any accumulated juices over the meat. Serve the sauce on the side.

Gilroy Smoked Tri-tip

Serves 6 to 8

Ingredients:

- 1 tri-tip roast (3 to 4 pounds)
- 1 tablespoon chili powder
- 1 teaspoon garlic salt
- Copious amounts of freshly ground black pepper
- Your favorite fresh salsa and pinto beans cooked with bacon for serving

Method:

1. At least 1 hour before cooking, remove the roast from the refrigerator. Season all sides with the chili powder, garlic salt, and lots and lots of black pepper.
2. Light a fire in the kamado grill using your favorite method. After about 10 minutes, close the dome and open the upper and lower dampers all the way. When the temperature reaches 300°F, place the wood chunks around the fire and add any accessories necessary for smoking on your particular grill, along with the grill rack. Close the dome, let the temperature build back to between 200° and 250°F, and wait for a little smoke to accumulate. Adjust the dampers to maintain the temperature in this range.
3. Place the roast on the grill and smoke until an instant-read thermometer registers between 130° and 140°F, about 2 hours. Transfer the roast to a cutting board, tent with aluminum foil, and let rest for 15 minutes. Slice very thinly against the grain. Arrange on a platter and pour any accumulated juice over the top. Serve with salsa and pinto beans.

Smoky Slab of Beef Ribs

Serves 4

Ingredients:

- 2 racks beef ribs, 8 bones each
- 1 tablespoon granulated garlic
- 1 teaspoon granulated onion
- 1 teaspoon dried thyme
- Kosher salt and freshly ground black pepper
- Your favorite barbecue sauce for serving

Method:

1. At least 1 hour before you're ready to grill, remove the ribs from the refrigerator. With a sharp knife, remove the thin membrane from the back of each rack and trim off any excess fat. Season the ribs on all sides with the garlic, onion, thyme, and a fairly generous amount of salt and pepper.
2. Light a fire in the kamado grill using your favorite method. After about 10 minutes, close the dome and open the upper and lower dampers all the way. When the temperature reaches 300°F, place the wood chunks around the fire and add any accessories necessary for smoking on your particular grill, along with the grill rack. Close the dome, let the temperature build back to between 200° and 250°F, and wait for a little smoke to accumulate. Adjust the dampers to maintain the temperature in this range.
3. Place the ribs, bone side down, on the grill, close the dome, and cook until tender, about 2 hours. The ribs are done when they're tender when poked with a knife and droop significantly when picked up with tongs.
4. Place the racks on a cutting board and let rest for 10 minutes. Slice off a rib and enjoy your "chef's treat." When you taste the rib, it should be tender but it still should take some bite to pull it off the bone. Cut into individual ribs and serve with barbecue sauce.

Jerk Chicken

Serves 4

Ingredients:

- 1 (4- to 5-pound) whole chicken
- 3/4 cup jerk marinade

Method:

1. Pat the chicken dry. Place it breast-side up on cutting board with the legs facing you, so the vity is visible. Using poultry shears, cut along the bottom of the cavity on each side of the backbone and neck to release them; remove and discard. Using the palms of your hands, flatten the breasts. Transfer to a shallow dish.
2. Pour the marinade over the chicken and rub it evenly into the flesh on both sides. Refrigerate overnight.
3. Prepare the grill for smoking at 225°F to 275°F.
4. Place the chicken skin-side up on the grate over the drip pan. Close the lid and cook for 2 hours 30 minutes to 3 hours or until an instant-read thermometer inserted into the center registers 600°F.
5. Rest for 10 minutes before serving. Carve off the breasts, thighs, legs, and wings; cut the breasts into slices and serve.

Pulled Pork Tacos With Charred Tomatillo Salsa

Serves 4

Ingredients:

- 6 cups carolina pulled pork
- 12 (5-inch) corn tortillas, warmed
- 1½ cups charred tomatillo salsa
- 1½ cups finely chopped fresh pineapple
- 3/4 cup finely chopped red onion
- 12 fresh cilantro sprigs

Method:

1. Divide the pulled pork among the warm tortillas.
2. Top each with 2 tablespoons of salsa, 2 tablespoons of pineapple, 1 tablespoon of onion, and 1 cilantro sprig. Serve immediately.

Chapter 3: Roasting

Classic Roast Chicken

Serves 4

Ingredients:

- 1 (4-to 5-pound) whole chicken
- Kosher salt
- Vegetable oil, for coating the chicken
- Freshly ground black pepper

Method:

1. Season the chicken generously with salt. Refrigerate overnight.
2. Pat the chicken dry.
3. Prepare the grill for roasting with a drip pan at 450°F.
4. Lightly coat the chicken with vegetable oil.
5. Place the chicken breast-side up on the grate over the drip pan. Close the lid and cook for 40 to 45 minutes or until an instant-read thermometer inserted into the thigh without touching the bone registers 160°F.
6. Season with pepper. Rest for 10 minutes. Carve off the breasts, thighs, legs, and wings; cut the breasts into slices and serve.

Roasted Rack Of Lamb With Thyme

Serves 4

Ingredients:

- 1/3 cup Dijon mustard
- 2 tablespoons ketchup
- 1 tablespoon Worcestershire sauce
- 1 tablespoon fresh lemon juice
- 1/4 cup chopped fresh thyme or lemon thyme (preferred)
- 2 (1½-pound) racks of lamb, Frenched if desired
- 1/4 cup olive oil

Method:

1. In a small bowl, whisk the mustard, ketchup, Worcestershire, lemon juice, and thyme together, then brush the mixture liberally over the lamb. Cover with plastic wrap and refrigerate overnight. Reserve the remaining marinade.
2. Wipe the marinade off the lamb, then brush the lamb with the olive oil.
3. Light a fire in the kamado grill using your favorite method. After about 10 minutes, place the grill rack in position, close the dome, and open the upper and lower dampers all the way. When the temperature reaches 500°F, adjust the dampers to maintain the temperature.
4. Place the lamb on the grill and sear for a couple of minutes on each side. Remove the lamb from the grill and brush on both sides with the reserved marinade.
5. Insert the ceramic plate in the kamado and put the lamb back on the grill, or set the lamb racks in a roasting pan and set the pan on the grill. Close the dome and roast until the internal temperature reads 125°F, 20 to 30 minutes, brushing with the marinade again halfway through.
6. Transfer the racks to a cutting board and let rest at least 10 minutes before cutting into individual or double chops. Serve at once.

Charred Whole Beef Tenderloin With Romesco Sauce

Serves 8 to 10

Ingredients:

- 1/2 cup roasted red peppers
- 1/3 cup natural almonds
- 2 tablespoons red wine vinegar
- 1/2 teaspoon red pepper flakes
- 2 cloves garlic, peeled
- 1 slice sourdough bread, crust removed
- 1/4 cup extra-virgin olive oil
- 1 whole beef tenderloin (about 6½ pounds), silverskin removed (it's best to have your butcher remove this; unless you have a super-sharp knife, you're likely to lose some of the meat along with the silverskin)
- 6 cloves garlic, thinly sliced
- Kosher salt and freshly ground black pepper
- 12 green onions, trimmed

Method:

1. Place the roasted peppers, almonds, vinegar, red pepper flakes, whole garlic cloves, and bread in a blender and pulse to combine. With the machine running, add the oil slowly and process until you have a nice thick sauce. The Romesco sauce can be prepared a day ahead and refrigerated in an airtight container. Bring to room temperature before using.
2. Using a boning knife, cut small slits into the beef tenderloin and slide in the slices of garlic. Liberally season with salt and pepper. Let rest at room temperature for at least 45 minutes before cooking.
3. Light a fire in the kamado grill using your favorite method. After about 10 minutes, place the grill rack in position, close the dome, and open the upper and lower dampers all the way. When the temperature reaches 500°F, adjust the dampers to maintain the temperature.
4. Place the tenderloin on the grill, close the dome, and sear for 5 minutes per side.

5. Insert the ceramic plate in the kamado and put the tenderloin on the grill, or put the tenderloin on a rack in a roasting pan and put the pan on the grill. Throw the green onions on the grill as well. Close the dome. The temperature will have dropped to around 425 and 450°F; adjust the vents to maintain that temperature and continue to roast to your desired degree of doneness, 1 hour to 1 hour and 15 minutes for medium rare (an internal temperature of 135 and 145°F).
6. Transfer the tenderloin to a platter and let rest for at least 15 minutes. To serve, slice, arrange the green onions with the beef, and spoon the Romesco sauce over everything. This is delicious warm or at room temperature.

Cornish Game Hens With Jalapeño Pesto

Serves 4

Ingredients:

- 2 jalapeño chiles, peeled (see below) and seeded
- 2 cups lightly packed fresh cilantro leaves
- 1 clove garlic, peeled
- 1/2 cup blanched almonds
- 1/4 cup (about 1 ounce) crumbled cotija cheese (available at most supermarkets and Hispanic markets)
- 1/4 cup extra-virgin olive oil
- 2 tablespoons fresh lemon juice
- Kosher salt and freshly ground black pepper
- 4 (1½-pound) Cornish game hens, defrosted if necessary

Method:

1. In a food processor or blender, combine the chiles, cilantro, garlic, and almonds and pulse until chopped, scraping down the sides once or twice during the process. Add the cheese and puree. With the motor running, add the olive oil and lemon juice. Transfer the pesto to a bowl and taste for seasoning, adding salt and pepper if necessary. Cover and refrigerate until needed. This can be made several hours in advance.
2. When ready, remove about 1/3 cup of the pesto to a separate bowl. Using an iced tea spoon or other small spoon and your finger, loosen the skin around the breast and the thigh of the game hens. Take a spoonful of pesto and push it up under the skin of both the breast and thigh, repeating for the other side and the other birds.
3. Light a fire in the kamado grill using your favorite method. After about 10 minutes, place the grill rack in position, close the dome, and open the upper and lower dampers all the way. When the temperature reaches 400°F, adjust the dampers to maintain the temperature.
4. Insert the ceramic plate in the kamado and put the hens on the grill, or put the hens on a rack in a roasting pan and put the pan on the grill. Close the dome and

roast the birds until the juice runs clear and the internal temperature at the thigh registers 165°F, 45 to 75 minutes.

5. Transfer the hens to a platter and let rest for 15 minutes before serving. Serve with the remaining pesto on the side.

Cauliflower With Olives And Toasted Bread Crumbs

Serves 4

Ingredients:

- 1 head cauliflower, cut into florets
- 1 tablespoon vegetable oil
- Kosher salt
- Freshly ground black pepper
- 2 tablespoons plain bread crumbs
- 10 pitted kalamata olives, thinly sliced
- Extra-virgin olive oil, for serving

Method:

1. Prepare the grill for roasting at 475°F, then preheat a 10-inch cast iron skillet on the grate with the grill lid closed.
2. In a large bowl, toss the cauliflower with the vegetable oil until coated. Season with salt and pepper; toss again. Transfer to the skillet.
3. Close the grill lid and cook for 15 to 20 minutes or until the cauliflower is tender and browned around the edges. When it looks nearly done, scatter the bread crumbs on top and finish cooking.
4. Transfer to a serving dish. Scatter the olives over the top, drizzle with olive oil, and serve immediately.

Everyday Roasted Chicken

Serves 4 to 6

Ingredients:

- 1 (4-pound) chicken
- No-salt-added seasoned "salt"
- Kosher salt and freshly ground black pepper
- OR
- 2 cups Herb Poultry Marinade

Method:

1. Remove the giblets and neck from the chicken's cavity and freeze for another use. Rinse the chicken thoroughly in cold water and pat dry with paper towels. Sprinkle inside and out liberally with the seasoned "salt," salt, and pepper, place on a rack in a roasting pan, and refrigerate overnight. OR, place the chicken in a 2½-gallon zip-top plastic bag and add the marinade. Seal the bag, turn it over several times to coat the chicken with the marinade, and refrigerate at least overnight and up to 2 days, turning the bag occasionally.
2. Remove the chicken from the refrigerator 30 minutes before cooking. Tie the legs together with kitchen twine, and flip the wing tips under the breast. If necessary, remove the chicken from the marinade.
3. Light a fire in the kamado grill using your favorite method. After about 10 minutes, place the grill rack in position, close the dome, and open the upper and lower dampers all the way. When the temperature reaches 400°F, adjust the dampers to maintain the temperature.
4. Insert the ceramic plate in the kamado and set the chicken on the grill, or set the chicken on a rack in a roasting pan and place the roasting pan on the grill. Close the dome and roast until the juices run clear and the internal temperature at the thigh is 170°F, about 1 to 1½ hours.
5. Transfer to a platter and let rest for 10 minutes before cutting into serving pieces.

Bok Choy With Soy, Sesame, And Garlic

Serves 4

Ingredients:

- 2½ pounds baby bok choy, quartered
- Lengthwise
- 2 teaspoons vegetable oil
- 3 garlic cloves, grated
- 2 tablespoons soy sauce
- 2 teaspoons sesame seeds

Method:

1. Prepare the grill for roasting at 425°F.
2. In a large bowl, toss the bok choy with the oil to coat.
3. Put the bok choy on the grate. Close the lid and cook, turning halfway through, for about 5 minutes total or until the leaves are charred and the stems are crisp-tender. Transfer to a bowl.
4. Toss with the garlic, soy sauce, and sesame seeds. Serve immediately.

Your Goose Is Cooked

Serves 6

Ingredients:

- 1 (9- to 11-pound) goose
- 1 orange, cut in half
- 1 teaspoon ground allspice
- Kosher salt and freshly ground black pepper
- 1/2 cup maple syrup (grade B preferred)
- 1/4 cup orange-flavored liqueur

Method:

1. Remove the giblets and any obvious fat from the goose. With an ice pick or metal skewer, puncture the skin of the goose all over. This will let excess fat render out of the goose. Rub the orange halves all over the goose, inside and out, squeezing the juice out as you do. Place the orange halves inside the cavity. Season the goose inside and out with the allspice and salt and pepper to taste. Cover with plastic wrap and refrigerate for 24 hours.
2. Remove the bird from the refrigerator at least 1 hour before you plan to roast. Cross the legs and tie them together with kitchen twine and put the wing joints under the bird. Place the bird on a rack in a roasting pan.
3. Light a fire in the kamado grill using your favorite method. After about 10 minutes, place the grill rack in position, close the dome, and open the upper and lower dampers all the way. When the temperature reaches 500°F, adjust the dampers to maintain the temperature.
4. Place the roasting pan on the grill, close the dome, and roast for about 30 minutes.
5. Adjust the dampers to drop the grill temperature to 350°F. Roast for 1 hour, then baste with the maple syrup. Roast for about another hour, basting every 30 minutes, alternating between the maple syrup and pan juices each time. The bird is done when the juices run clear and the internal temperature at the thigh is 165°F; figure on 20 minutes per pound.
6. Transfer the goose to a cutting board and let rest for 15 minutes before carving.

Broccoli With Lemon Zest And Parmesan

Serves 4

Ingredients:

- 1 head broccoli, cut into florets
- 2 teaspoons vegetable oil
- Grated zest of 1 lemon
- Kosher salt
- Freshly ground black pepper
- 1/4 cup grated parmesan cheese
- Extra-virgin olive oil, for serving

Method:

1. Prepare the grill for roasting at 475°F, then preheat a 10-inch cast iron skillet on the grate with the grill lid closed.
2. In a large bowl, toss the broccoli with the vegetable oil until coated. Add the lemon zest and season with salt and pepper; toss again. Transfer to the skillet.
3. Close the grill lid and cook for 15 to 20 minutes or until the broccoli is tender and browned around the edges. Transfer to a serving dish.
4. Sprinkle with the Parmesan, drizzle with olive oil, and serve immediately.

Greek Potato Wedges

Serves 4

Ingredients:

- 2 large russet potatoes, each cut into six wedges
- 1 tablespoon vegetable oil
- Kosher salt
- 1 teaspoon dried oregano
- 2 ounces feta, crumbled

Method:

1. Prepare the grill for roasting at 475°F.
2. In a large bowl, toss the potatoes with the oil until coated. Season with salt and the oregano; toss again.
3. Put the potato wedges on the grate. Close the lid and cook for 20 to 25 minutes or until crispy and brown on the outside and fluffy and tender on the inside.
4. Transfer to a serving dish. Top with the feta and serve immediately.

Marinated Herb-Mustard Leg of Lamb

Serves 6 to 8

Ingredients:

- 1 (4-to 5-pound) boneless or 1 (6-to 8-pound) bone-in leg of lamb
- 3/4 cup vegetable oil
- 1/2 cup red wine vinegar
- 1/2 cup chopped onion
- 2 cloves garlic, bruised
- 2 teaspoons Dijon mustard
- 2 teaspoons kosher salt
- 1/2 teaspoon dried oregano
- 1/2 teaspoon dried basil
- 1 bay leaf
- 1/8 teaspoon freshly ground black pepper

Method:

1. If working with a bone-in leg, have your butcher bone the leg and butterfly it. Place the lamb in a 2½-gallon zip-top plastic bag.
2. In a medium bowl, whisk the oil, vinegar, onion, garlic, mustard, salt, oregano, basil, bay leaf, and pepper together. Add to the bag, seal, and squish the marinade all around to coat the lamb. Refrigerate for 48 hours, turning the bag over occasionally.
3. Remove the lamb from the marinade, reserving the marinade. Pat the lamb dry and let sit at room temperature for about 30 minutes. Bring the marinade to a full boil in a small saucepan over high heat. Reduce the heat slightly and cook for 5 minutes. Remove from the heat and let cool.
4. Light a fire in the kamado grill using your favorite method. After about 10 minutes, place the grill rack in position, close the dome, and open the upper and lower dampers all the way. When the temperature reaches 500°F, adjust the dampers to maintain the temperature.

5. Set the lamb on the grill, close the dome, and sear about 5 minutes per side. Remove the lamb from the grill.
6. Insert the ceramic plate in the kamado and put the lamb back on the grill, or set the lamb on a rack in a roasting pan and put the pan on the grill. Close the dome and adjust the dampers to drop the grill temperature to 350°F. Roast until the internal temperature at the thickest point of the lamb registers 135°F, about 1 to 1½ hours.
7. Transfer the lamb to a cutting board and let rest for 10 minutes. The lamb will be crusty on the outside and cooked to multiple levels of doneness, from rare to well done. Cut into slices and serve with the reserved marinade, reheated, as a dipping sauce.

Sunday-Best Pork Loin Roast With Thyme-Fig Balsamic Marinade

Serves 6 to 8

Ingredients:

- 3/4 cup fig balsamic vinegar
- 1/3 cup olive oil
- 6 cloves garlic, finely chopped
- 3 tablespoons chopped fresh thyme
- 1 tablespoon Dijon mustard
- 1 teaspoon kosher salt
- 1 teaspoon fennel seeds
- Freshly ground black pepper
- 1 (3- to 4-pound) center-cut boneless pork loin roast

Method:

1. In a small bowl, whisk the vinegar, oil, garlic, thyme, mustard, salt, fennel seeds, and 5 grindings of black pepper together. Place the pork roast in a 2½-gallon zip-top plastic bag. Add the marinade, seal the bag, and squish the marinade around the pork to coat. Refrigerate for at least 24 hours; 48 is better. Turn the bag frequently.
2. Remove the pork from the marinade at least 45 minutes before cooking; reserve the marinade. Let the pork stand at room temperature.
3. Light a fire in the kamado grill using your favorite method. After about 10 minutes, place the grill rack in position, close the dome, and open the upper and lower dampers all the way. When the temperature reaches 400°F, adjust the dampers to maintain the temperature.
4. Insert the ceramic plate in the kamado and place the roast on the grill, or set the pork roast on a rack in a roasting pan, and place the pan on the grill. Close the dome and adjust the dampers for a grill temperature of 375°F. Roast for about 20 minutes, then brush the pork with the reserved marinade. Cook for another 45 to 60 minutes for a medium doneness; the internal temperature should be between 145° and 150°F

5. Transfer the pork to a cutting board and let rest for 15 minutes. Cut into 1/2-inch-thick slices and serve warm or at room temperature.

Steakhouse Roast

Serves 6 to 8

Ingredients:

- 1 tablespoon Canadian-Style Steak Seasoning
- 1 tablespoon garlic paste (about 8 cloves garlic, smashed and worked into a paste, or prepared garlic paste in a tube, which can be found in the produce section)
- 1 tablespoon Worcestershire sauce
- 1 teaspoon Dijon mustard
- 1 (3- to 4-pound) New York strip loin roast
- Horseradish or steak sauce for serving

Method:

1. In a small bowl, combine the steak seasoning, garlic, Worcestershire, and mustard and massage the mixture into the roast. Set the roast on a rack in a roasting pan and let stand at room temperature for an hour.
2. Light a fire in the kamado grill using your favorite method. After about 10 minutes, place the grill rack in position, close the dome, and open the upper and lower dampers all the way. When the temperature reaches 500°F, adjust the dampers to maintain the temperatures.
3. Insert the ceramic plate in the kamado and put the roast on the grill, or put the roast on a rack in a roasting pan and put the pan on the grill. Close the dome and adjust the dampers for a grill temperature of 450°F. Roast to your desired degree of doneness, 1½ to 2 hours for medium rare (an internal temperature of 135° and 140°F).
4. Transfer the roast to a cutting board and let rest for 15 minutes. Slice as you prefer (I like 1/2-inch- thick slices), arrange on a platter, and serve with the sauces if desired.

Moroccan Roasted Carrots

Serves 4

Ingredients:

- 8 medium carrots (about 1½ pounds), peeled
- 1 teaspoon vegetable oil
- Kosher salt
- 1 tablespoon honey
- Juice of 1/4 lemon
- 1 tablespoon extra-virgin olive oil
- 1 teaspoon cumin seeds, toasted
- 1 tablespoon sesame seeds, toasted
- 10 fresh cilantro sprigs
- Freshly ground black pepper

Method:

1. Prepare the grill for roasting at 450°F.
2. On a baking sheet, toss the carrots with the vegetable oil to coat. Season with salt; toss again.
3. Put the carrots on the grate. Close the lid and cook for 15 to 20 minutes or until tender at the thickest point. Transfer to a plate and refrigerate.
4. Once just cool enough to handle, cut the carrots into 1-inch pieces on an angle. Transfer to a bowl.
5. Toss with the honey, lemon juice, olive oil, cumin and sesame seeds, and cilantro. Season with salt and pepper. Serve at room temperature or chilled.

Roasted Pork Loin Stuffed With Bacon-Onion Jam, Mascarpone, Apricots, And Plums

Serves 6 to 8

Ingredients:

- 1 (4- to 5 -pound) boneless center-cut pork loin roast
- 1/2 cup Bacon-Onion Jam or store-bought onion jam
- 1/2 cup mascarpone cheese
- 12 to 14 dried apricots
- 12 to 14 dried plums (prunes)
- Kosher salt and freshly ground black pepper
- Kitchen twine
- Apricot jam, slightly melted so it's easy to brush

Method:

1. Slice the pork roast lengthwise but not all the way through. Open the roast up and then slice both sides in half so that the pork roast lies open like a book. Take care not to cut any of the meat all the way through.
2. Smear the insides of the pork roast with the bacon-onion jam. Spread the mascarpone over the jam and then top with the apricots and dried plums, spreading them evenly throughout the roast. Season with salt and pepper. Roll the roast tightly together lengthwise and tie at 1-inch intervals with kitchen twine. Let sit at room temperature while you start your fire.
3. Light a fire in the kamado grill using your favorite method. After about 10 minutes, place the grill rack in position, close the dome, and open the upper and lower dampers all the way. When the temperature reaches 400°F, adjust the dampers to maintain the temperature.
4. Insert the ceramic plate in the kamado or set the roast on a rack in a roasting pan and place the pan on the grill. Close the dome and adjust the temperature downward to 375°F. Roast for about 1 hour, then brush with the apricot jam. Continue to cook about another 20 minutes, brushing again with the jam toward

the end of that time. The roast is ready when the internal temperature is between 140° and 150°F.

5. Transfer the pork to a cutting board and let rest for 15 minutes. Cut into 1/2-inch-thick slices and serve warm or at room temperature.

Pollo A La Brasa

Serves 4

Ingredients:

- 8 garlic cloves, peeled
- 1/2 cup soy sauce
- Juice of 1/4 lime
- 2 tablespoons vegetable oil
- 2 teaspoons dried oregano
- 2 teaspoons cumin seeds
- 1 teaspoon sweet paprika
- 1/4 teaspoon cayenne pepper
- 1 (4- to 5-pound) whole chicken
- 3/4 cup peruvian cilantro sauce

Method:

1. Put the garlic, soy sauce, lime juice, oil, oregano, cumin seeds, paprika, and cayenne in the bowl of a food processor. Blend until combined.
2. Put the chicken in a shallow dish and pour the marinade over. Rub evenly into the flesh on both sides. Refrigerate overnight.
3. Prepare the grill for roasting at 450°F.
4. Put the chicken breast-side up on the grate. Close the lid and cook for 40 to 45 minutes or until an instant-read thermometer inserted into the thigh without touching the bone registers 160°F.
5. Rest for 10 minutes. Carve off the breasts, thighs, legs, and wings; cut the breast into slices and serve with the sauce on the side.

Baku Eggplant Salad

Serves 4

Ingredients:

- 1 large italian eggplant
- 1/2 teaspoon vegetable oil
- 1/2 pint grape tomatoes, finely diced
- 1/2 green bell pepper, seeded and finely diced
- 1 persian cucumber, finely diced
- 1/4 red onion, finely diced
- Juice of 1 lemon
- 1 tablespoon extra-virgin olive oil
- 1/2 teaspoon smoked paprika
- Kosher salt
- Freshly ground black pepper

Method:

1. Prepare the grill for roasting at 550°F.
2. Using a fork, poke holes in several places on the eggplant. Coat with the vegetable oil.
3. Put the eggplant on the grate. Close the lid and cook for 15 to 20 minutes or until charred and the flesh pulls away from the skin. Transfer to a plate and refrigerate.
4. Once cool enough to handle, halve the eggplant lengthwise; scoop the flesh into a large bowl.
5. Stir in the tomatoes, bell pepper, cucumber, onion, lemon juice, olive oil, and paprika. Season with salt and pepper. Serve chilled.

Cuban Roast Pork (Pernil)

Serves 16

Ingredients:

- 1 (8-to 9-pound) bone-in, skin-on pork shoulder roast
- Kosher salt
- 1 recipe mojo marinade

Method:

1. With a small sharp knife, make 1-inch-deep cuts all over the pork. Season generously with salt. Place in a large nonreactive container and rub all over with the marinade. Refrigerate overnight.
2. Prepare the grill for roasting with a drip pan at 350°F.
3. Place the pork fat-side up on the grate over the drip pan. Close the lid and cook for 2 hours 45 minutes to 3 hours or until an instant-read thermometer inserted into the thickest part away from the bone registers 190°F
4. Transfer the roast to a large cutting board. When it cools enough to comfortably handle, remove the bones and chop or shred (which you can do with two forks) the meat. Chop the crisp skin and mix it in with the meat.

Roasted Side Of Salmon With Herb Goat Cheese And Spinach

Serves 8

Ingredients:

- 10 ounces fresh spinach leaves, well washed and trimmed of heavy stems
- 4 ounces herb-flavored goat cheese, at room temperature
- Pinch of freshly grated nutmeg
- Kosher salt and freshly ground black pepper
- 1 (4-pound) side of salmon
- Olive oil for brushing
- 2 cups plain dry breadcrumbs
- 1/2 cup (1 stick) unsalted butter, melted

Method:

1. Blanch the spinach in a pot of boiling salted water until wilted, about 30 seconds. Drain and rinse with cold water. Roll the spinach up in paper towels and squeeze to get out as much water out as possible. Finely chop the spinach and put in a bowl. Add the goat cheese, nutmeg, salt, and pepper and stir until well combined.
2. Cut a 1/2-inch-deep pocket along the top of the salmon, running its entire length. Use your fingers to open the pocket and stuff as much of the spinach mixture into the pocket as possible. Mound the rest on top of the salmon. Brush a rimmed baking sheet with olive oil. Place the salmon on the baking sheet.
3. Light a fire in the kamado grill using your favorite method. After about 10 minutes, place the grill rack in position, close the dome, and open the upper and lower dampers all the way. When the temperature reaches 600°F, adjust the dampers to maintain the temperature.
4. Toss the breadcrumbs and melted butter together and sprinkle over the top of the salmon to form a crust. Place the baking pan on the grill and close the dome. Roast until the tip of a cake tester stuck into the thickest part of the salmon is just warm when touched to your lip, about 12 minutes.
5. Remove the pan from the kamado and, using two long spatulas, transfer the salmon to a platter, and serve.

Papas Con Rajas

Serves 4

Ingredients:

- 5 yukon gold potatoes, cut into 1-inch dice (about 1½ pounds)
- 1 red onion, cut into 1-inch dice
- 3 large poblano peppers
- 1 tablespoon vegetable oil
- Kosher salt

Method:

1. Prepare the grill for roasting at 475°F, then preheat a 10-inch cast iron skillet on the grate with the grill lid closed.
2. In a large bowl, toss the potatoes, onion, and peppers with the oil to coat. Season with salt.
3. Put the potatoes and onion in the skillet. Put the peppers on the grate. Close the grill lid and cook, turning occasionally, for 15 to 20 minutes or until the peppers are charred on all sides. Transfer the peppers to a paper bag to steam.
4. Continue cooking the potatoes and onion for 10 to 15 more minutes or until they are fork-tender and browned around the edges. Remove from the heat.
5. Remove the peppers from the bag. Once cool enough to handle, slip off the skins and cut into thin strips, discarding the stems and seeds. Toss with the onion and potatoes. Serve immediately.

Chapter 4: Steaming & Braising

New England Shore Dinner Without The Shore

Serves 8

Ingredients:

- 16 small new red potatoes
- 8 small onions, peeled
- 3 bunches fresh thyme
- 5 pounds cherrystone clams, cleaned
- 8 ears corn, shucked, silks removed, and broken in half
- 2 pounds mussels, debearded
- 4 cups bottled clam juice
- 4 cups water
- 8 lobster tails (4 to 6 ounces each), thawed if necessary
- 6 or more lemons cut into wedges for serving
- Unsalted butter, melted, for serving
- Cocktail sauce for serving
- Sliced crusty peasant bread for dipping in the broth

Method:

1. Place the potatoes and onions in a large, deep roasting pan, like a turkey roaster. Scatter about one-third of the thyme over the vegetables. Arrange the clams evenly over the vegetables, then set the corn on top. Spread the mussels around the corn and scatter the remaining thyme on top.
2. Light a fire in the kamado grill using your favorite method. After about 10 minutes, place the grill rack in position, close the dome, and open the upper and lower dampers all the way. When the temperature reaches 400°F, adjust the dampers to maintain the temperature.
3. Pour the clam juice and water in the pan. Cover with aluminum foil, place on the grill, and close the dome. Let steam for 10 to 15 minutes.

4. Set the lobster tails on top of the other ingredients, recover with the foil, close the dome, and cook until their meat is firm at the exposed end, another 15 minutes.
5. Bring the roasting pan to a table covered with several layers of newspaper. Put out the lemons, butter, cocktail sauce, and bread and let everybody dig in.

Steamed Tilefish With Orange, Ginger, And Green Onions

Serves 6

Ingredients:

- 3 tablespoons orange juice
- 2 teaspoons grated orange zest
- 2 tablespoons olive oil
- 2 tablespoons white wine
- 2 cloves garlic, minced
- 1 (2-inch) piece fresh ginger, peeled and cut into matchsticks
- 1/4 cup chopped green onions
- 2 tablespoons chopped fresh flat-leaf parsley
- 6 (4-to 6-ounce) tilefish fillets
- Kosher salt and freshly ground black pepper
- Thin orange slices

Method:

1. Cut six 10-inch squares of heavy-duty aluminum foil.
2. In a small bowl, whisk the orange juice and zest, oil, wine, and garlic together until blended. Stir in the ginger, green onions, and parsley.
3. Season the fillets with salt and pepper. Place one fillet in each center of the sheet of foil. Pour the orange mixture evenly over the fillets. Top each fillet with orange slices. Fold the foil over the fish and press to seal the edges tightly.
4. Light a fire in the kamado grill using your favorite method. After about 10 minutes, place the grill rack in position, close the dome, and open the upper and lower dampers all the way. When the temperature reaches 400°F, adjust the dampers to maintain the temperature.
5. Place the packets on the grill and close the dome. Grill for 8 minutes.
6. Transfer each packet to a serving plate. Let each diner cut into their own packet to experience the intoxicating smell of the wonderful steam.

Kamado Brunswick Stew

Serves 15 to 18

Ingredients:

- 1 cup (2 sticks) unsalted butter
- 3 cups finely diced onions (about 2 large)
- 2 tablespoons finely chopped garlic
- 1 tablespoon freshly ground black pepper
- 1 cup Lexington-Style "Dip"
- 1/4 cup Worcestershire sauce
- 1/4 cup yellow mustard
- 1/4 cup honey
- 1 pound leftover boneless smoked pork
- 1 pound leftover boneless smoked beef
- 1 pound leftover smoked poultry
- 2 (28-ounce) cans crushed tomatoes
- 3 cups fresh corn kernels (from 4 to 6 ears)
- 4 cups baby butter beans (lima beans)
- 2 quarts unsalted or low-sodium chicken broth
- Kosher salt
- 2 cups mashed potatoes
- Proper Cornbread
- Your favorite hot sauce

Method:

1. Light a fire in the kamado grill using your favorite method. After about 10 minutes, place the grill rack in position, close the dome, and open the upper and lower dampers all the way. When the temperature reaches 300°F, adjust the dampers to maintain the temperature.
2. Set the largest cast-iron Dutch oven pot you have on the stove over medium heat and melt the butter. Add the onions and garlic and cook, stirring a few times, until softened, 5 to 10 minutes. Stir in the pepper, dip, Worcestershire, mustard, and

honey and heat through. Stir in the meat, poultry, tomatoes, corn, beans, and broth and heat through.

3. Place the pot on the grill, close the dome, and let simmer for 2 to 3 hours, stirring occasionally. Taste the stew after 2 hours and see if it's to your liking. You might want to add some salt at this point and then taste again. You want a deep flavor with sweet, smoky notes. If the flavor's right, stir in the mashed potatoes, close the dome, and cook for another 30 minutes. I highly encourage you to wait at least 3 hours and, if you have the patience, up to 4 hours, before considering the stew done.

4. Remove the pot from the grill, ladle the stew into bowls, and serve with cornbread and hot sauce, if desired.

Italian-Style Braised Rabbit

Serves 4

Ingredients:

- 1 dressed rabbit (about 2½ pounds), thawed if necessary and cut into serving pieces
- Kosher salt and freshly ground black pepper
- 1/4 cup olive oil
- 1 cup chopped onion
- 2 ribs celery, diced
- 4 cloves garlic, chopped
- 1/2 cup dry white wine
- 1 tablespoon balsamic vinegar
- 2 cups unsalted or low-sodium broth
- 1 cup diced tomatoes (canned is fine)
- 1 teaspoon dried rosemary
- 1 teaspoon dried thyme
- 1/2 teaspoon dried oregano
- 1/2 cup chopped fresh parsley

Method:

1. Light a fire in the kamado grill using your favorite method. After about 10 minutes, place the grill rack in position, close the dome, and open the upper and lower dampers all the way. When the temperature reaches 400°F, adjust the dampers to maintain the temperature.
2. Season the rabbit pieces generously with salt and pepper. Place the rabbit on the grill, close the dome, and sear until nicely browned, about 3 minutes per side. Transfer to a platter.
3. Place a Dutch oven on the grill, add the olive oil, close the dome, and let the oil heat for about 2 minutes. Throw in the onion and celery, close the dome, and cook for 2 minutes, then stir in the garlic. Place the rabbit back in the pot, add the wine and vinegar, close the dome, bring to a boil (which should take about 5

minutes), and let boil for 2 minutes. Pour in the broth and tomatoes and stir in the dried herbs. Cover the pot, close the dome, adjust the dampers to maintain a temperature of 350° to 375°F, and braise until the rabbit is fork tender, 1 to 1½ hours.

4. Remove the pot from the kamado and stir in the fresh parsley. Taste the broth for salt and pepper, and adjust as needed. Let rest, covered, for at least 20 minutes to let the flavors develop. Serve the rabbit topped with the braising liquid and vegetables.

Pork Osso Buco

Serves 6

Ingredients:

- 1 cup dry white wine
- 1/2 cup bourbon
- 1/4 cup molasses
- 1/4 cup cider vinegar
- 10 cloves garlic, peeled and smashed
- 8 sprigs fresh thyme
- 6 bay leaves
- 4 sprigs fresh rosemary
- 6 slices pork shank, 1½ to 2 inches thick, skin removed
- Kosher salt and freshly ground black pepper
- Low-sodium or unsalted chicken broth as needed
- Cooked grits, pinto beans, or garlic mashed potatoes for serving
- 1 cup chowchow

Method:

1. Combine the wine, bourbon, molasses, and vinegar, then stir to combine. Throw in the garlic, thyme, bay leaves, and rosemary. Place the pork in 2-gallon zip-top plastic bag. Add the marinade, seal, and refrigerate for at least 24 hours, turning the bag over several times.
2. Remove the pork from the refrigerator at least 1 hour before cooking. Take the pork from the bag, reserving the marinade, and pat dry. Season liberally with salt and pepper.
3. Light a fire in the kamado grill using your favorite method. After about 10 minutes, place the grill rack in position, close the dome, and open the upper and lower dampers all the way. When the temperature reaches 400°F, adjust the dampers to maintain the temperature.
4. Place the pork on the grill, close the dome, and sear until nicely browned, 3 to 4 minutes per side. Transfer the pork to a large cast-iron Dutch oven, add the

reserved marinade, and add enough broth to come even with the top of the pork. Cover. Adjust the dampers to drop the temperature in the kamado to 350°F.

5. Place the pan on the grill, close the dome, and braise the pork until it is super tender, about 2 hours. There should be no resistance when you insert a knife into a thickest section of the pork, and the juices should run clear.

6. Transfer the pork to a plate and tent with aluminum foil. Strain the braising liquid through a fine mesh strainer into a saucepan and bring to a boil. Cook over medium heat until the sauce is reduced by half, usually about 10 minutes. (At this point, you can cover and refrigerate the pork and liquid for up to 2 days. When ready to use, defat both the pork and liquid. Gently rewarm the pork in the broth.)

7. To serve, place a mound of grits, pinto beans, or potatoes in the bottom of a shallow soup bowl. Place one piece of pork on top and divide the chowchow among the servings. Spoon the reduced braising liquid around the pork and serve immediately.

Mussels With Shallots, Tomatoes, And Basil

Serves 4

Ingredients:

- 2 tablespoons olive oil
- 3 tablespoons finely chopped shallots
- 1 tablespoon chopped garlic
- 2 pounds mussels (about 60), debearded
- 3/4 cup Riesling wine
- 1/4 cup fresh lemon juice
- 1/4 cup low-sodium chicken broth
- 1/4 cup diced plum tomatoes or drained canned diced tomatoes (if you're using canned and really like tomatoes, it won't hurt to use a whole 14.5- ounce can, drained)
- 1/4 cup (1/2 stick) unsalted butter, cut into small pieces
- Kosher salt and freshly ground black pepper
- 3 tablespoons thinly sliced fresh basil

Method:

1. In a medium skillet over medium heat, heat the oil until it begins to shimmer. Add the shallots and garlic and cook, stirring several times, until soft, about 3 minutes. Pour this mixture into a deep disposable aluminum-foil pan.
2. Light a fire in the kamado grill using your favorite method. After about 10 minutes, place the grill rack in position, close the dome, and open the upper and lower dampers all the way. When the temperature reaches 400°F, adjust the dampers to maintain the temperature.
3. Add the mussels, wine, lemon juice, broth, and tomatoes to the pan. Cover with aluminum foil, place on the grill, and close the dome. Steam until the mussels have opened, about 10 minutes.
4. Remove the pan from the grill and discard any mussels that have not opened. Add the butter to the pan, stirring to blend it with the broth. Season to taste with salt

and pepper, sprinkle in the basil, and toss. Divide the mussels and broth among 4 bowls and serve immediately.

Braised Leeks In Parmesan Cream

Serves 4

Ingredients:

- 3 or 4 large leeks
- 2 tablespoons extra-virgin olive oil, divided
- 1/4 cup low-sodium chicken broth
- 1/2 cup heavy cream
- 1 cup coarsely grated parmesan cheese, plus more for garnish
- Kosher salt
- Freshly ground black pepper

Method:

1. Cut off and discard the tough green tops and root ends of the leeks so you have lengths of white bulbs about 5 inches long. Halve each piece lengthwise and rinse thoroughly under running water to wash away any grit from between the layers. Dry thoroughly with paper towels.
2. Bring the grill to 400°F with the cooking grate and heat deflector installed, then preheat a 10-inch cast iron skillet on the grate with the lid closed.
3. Pour 1 tablespoon of oil into the skillet. Once hot, add half the leeks to the skillet, cut-side down and in a single layer. Close the lid and cook, undisturbed, for 5 to 7 minutes or until lightly browned. Transfer to a plate. Repeat with the remaining 1 tablespoon of oil and remaining leeks. Transfer to the same plate.
4. Add the broth, cream, and Parmesan (in that order) and stir until the cheese is melted. Season with salt and pepper. Add the leeks, turning to coat them in the cream. Cover the skillet with a tight-fitting lid. Close the grill lid and cook for 10 minutes.
5. Remove the lid from the skillet. Close the grill lid and cook for another 3 to 5 minutes or until the liquid has thickened slightly and the leeks are tender. Season with salt and pepper. Garnish with more Parmesan, if desired. Serve immediately.

Chicago-Style Italian Beef Sandwiches

Serves 8 to 10 or more

Ingredients:

- 1 teaspoon kosher salt
- 1 teaspoon freshly ground black pepper
- 1 teaspoon dried oregano
- 1 teaspoon dried basil
- 1 teaspoon dried parsley
- 1 teaspoon onion powder
- 1 teaspoon garlic powder
- 1 bay leaf
- 1 (2/3-ounce) package dry zesty Italian salad seasoning mix
- 3 cups low-sodium beef broth
- 1 (5-pound) eye of round roast
- Italian or Chicago rolls
- Giardiniera

Method:

1. Place all the seasonings and the broth in a large cast-iron Dutch oven. Stir to blend, then put in the roast. It's okay if you need to cut it in half. Cover.
2. Light a fire in the kamado grill using your favorite method. After about 10 minutes, place the grill rack in position, close the dome, and open the upper and lower dampers all the way. When the temperature reaches 350°F, adjust the dampers to maintain the temperature.
3. Place the Dutch oven on the grill, close the dome, and braise until the meat is fork tender, 3 to 4 hours.
4. Remove the Dutch oven from the kamado and discard the bay leaf. Shred the meat with a fork right in the pot with the juices. The meat juices are a big part of the sandwich. Serve on toasted Chicago or Italian rolls with giardiniera on the side and plenty of napkins.

Red Wine-Braised Short Ribs

Serves 4

Ingredients:

- 2 pounds bone-in beef short ribs
- Kosher salt
- 1 teaspoon vegetable oil
- 1 medium onion, coarsely chopped
- 3 medium carrots, coarsely chopped
- Freshly ground black pepper
- 2 cups red wine
- 2 cups low-sodium beef broth
- 10 fresh thyme sprigs
- 2 bay leaves

Method:

1. Season the beef generously with salt. Refrigerate overnight.
2. Pat the beef dry.
3. Bring the grill to 500°F with the cooking grate installed, then preheat a 5-quart cast iron Dutch oven on the grate with the grill lid closed.
4. Pour the oil into the Dutch oven and close the grill lid. Once hot, add the beef in a single layer. Close the grill lid and cook, turning every 5 to 6 minutes, for 20 to 24 minutes total or until browned on all sides. Transfer to a plate.
5. Add the onion and carrots to the Dutch oven. Close the grill lid and cook for 8 to 10 minutes or until softened. Season with salt and pepper.
6. Pour in the wine and broth to deglaze: Close the grill lid, bring to a boil, and gently scrape the bottom of the Dutch oven with a wooden spoon to loosen any browned bits.
7. Add the thyme and bay leaves. Close the grill lid and cook for 13 to 15 minutes or until the liquid is reduced by half, then add the beef. Cover the Dutch oven with a tight-fitting lid. Remove from the heat.

8. Wearing barbecue gloves, carefully remove the grate, install the heat deflector, and replace the grate. Reduce the grill temperature to 350°F.
9. Put the Dutch oven back on the grate. Close the grill lid and cook for 2 hours to 2 hours 30 minutes or until the beef is fork-tender.
10. Rest for 20 minutes before serving.

Orange-Braised Endive With Kalamata Olives

Serves 4

Ingredients:

- 2 tablespoons unsalted butter, divided
- 5 belgian endive, quartered lengthwise
- 3/4 cup freshly squeezed orange juice (from about 3 oranges)
- 1/4 cup low-sodium chicken broth
- Grated zest of 1 orange
- 1/2 cup pitted kalamata olives
- Kosher salt
- Freshly ground black pepper

Method:

1. Bring the grill to 400°F with the cooking grate and heat deflector installed, then preheat a 10-inch cast iron skillet on the grate with the lid closed.
2. Put 1 tablespoon of butter in the skillet and close the lid. When melted, add half the endive, cut-side down. Close the lid and cook, undisturbed, for about 10 minutes or until lightly browned. Transfer to a plate. Repeat with the remaining 1 tablespoon of butter and remaining endive.
3. Add the first batch of endive back to the skillet with the second batch. Pour in the orange juice and broth, and top with the orange zest. Cover the skillet with a tight-fitting lid. Close the grill lid and cook for 20 minutes.
4. Remove the lid from the skillet. Add the olives. Close the grill lid and cook for 10 minutes or until the liquid has thickened into a glaze. Season with salt and pepper. Serve immediately.

Aloo Gobi

Serves 6

Ingredients:

- 1 tablespoon vegetable oil
- 1 head cauliflower, cut into florets
- 1 medium russet potato, peeled and cut into 1-inch dice
- Kosher salt
- 1 tablespoon unsalted butter
- 2 teaspoons cumin seeds
- 1 medium red onion, finely diced
- 4 garlic cloves, finely chopped
- 1 (1-inch) piece fresh ginger, peeled and finely chopped
- 1 jalapeño pepper, stemmed and finely chopped
- 1 tablespoon garam masala
- 2 teaspoons ground coriander
- 1/2 teaspoon turmeric
- 1/4 teaspoon cayenne pepper
- 2 cups water

Method:

1. Bring the grill to 400°F with the cooking grate and heat deflector installed, then preheat a 5-quart cast iron Dutch oven on the grate with the grill lid closed.
2. Pour the oil into the Dutch oven and close the grill lid. When hot, add the cauliflower and potato in a single layer (you'll need to do this in two batches). Close the grill lid and cook, stirring occasionally, for 8 to 10 minutes or until lightly browned. Season with salt. Transfer to a plate.
3. Add the butter and close the grill lid. When melted, add the cumin seeds. Close the grill lid and cook for about 15 seconds or until they start to pop.
4. Add the onion and stir to combine. Close the grill lid and cook, stirring occasionally, for 2 to 3 minutes or until it starts to brown. Season with salt.

5. Add the garlic and ginger. Cook, stirring frequently, for 30 to 60 seconds or until fragrant.
6. Add the jalapeño, garam masala, coriander, turmeric, and cayenne and stir to combine. Close the grill lid and cook for 3 to 5 minutes or until the jalapeño has softened and the spices are toasted. Season with salt.
7. Add the cauliflower, potato, and water. Season with salt. Stir until thoroughly combined. Cover the Dutch oven with a tight-fitting lid. Close the grill lid and cook for 25 to 30 minutes or until the vegetables are very tender. Serve immediately or at room temperature.

Braised Lamb Shanks

Serves 6

Ingredients:

- 4 tablespoons olive oil
- 1 cup diced onion
- 5 cloves garlic, peeled and crushed
- 4 ribs celery, cut into 1/2-inch-thick slices
- 2 medium carrots, cut into 1/2-inch-thick rounds
- 2 cups dry red wine
- 2 bay leaves
- 6 oil-packed anchovy fillets
- 2 cups low-sodium beef broth
- 1 (32-ounce) can plum tomatoes, drained
- 10 black peppercorns
- 6 (1-to 1¼-pound) lamb shanks
- Kosher salt and freshly ground black pepper

Method:

1. In a large skillet over medium heat, heat 2 tablespoons of the oil, then add the onion, garlic, celery, and carrots and cook, stirring a few times, until the vegetables have slightly softened, 3 to 5 minutes. Add 1 cup of the wine and stir, scraping up any browned bits from the bottom of the skillet. Pour the contents of the skillet into a large disposable aluminum-foil pan. Add the remaining 1 cup wine, the bay leaves, anchovies, broth, tomatoes, and peppercorns.
2. Light a fire in the kamado grill using your favorite method. After about 10 minutes, place the grill rack in position, close the dome, and open the upper and lower dampers all the way. When the temperature reaches 325°F, adjust the dampers to maintain the temperature.
3. Brush the lamb shanks with the remaining 2 tablespoons oil and season with salt and pepper. Place the shanks on the grill, close the dome, and sear until nicely browned on all sides, turning the shanks every 2 to 3 minutes.

4. Transfer the lamb shanks to the foil pan, cover with foil, and set the pan on the grill. Close the dome and adjust the dampers to drop the temperature in the kamado down to about 325°F. Braise until the meat is exceedingly tender, about 2½ hours.
5. Transfer the shanks to a platter and cover with foil. Strain the braising liquid through a finemesh strainer into a medium saucepan. Bring to a boil and reduce until nicely thickened. Pour the sauce over the lamb shanks and serve.

Classic Beef Stew

Serves 8

Ingredients:

- 2 pounds boneless beef chuck roast, cut into 2-inch pieces
- Kosher salt
- 1 teaspoon vegetable oil
- 1 medium onion, coarsely chopped
- 2 medium carrots, coarsely chopped
- 2 celery stalks, coarsely chopped
- 3 garlic cloves, coarsely chopped
- Freshly ground black pepper
- 2 tablespoons tomato paste
- 3 cups low-sodium beef broth
- 2 bay leaves
- 1 pound red potatoes, quartered

Method:

1. Season the beef generously with salt. Refrigerate overnight.
2. Pat the beef dry.
3. Bring the grill to 500°F with the cooking grate installed, then preheat a 5-quart cast iron Dutch oven on the grate with the grill lid closed.
4. Pour the oil into the Dutch oven and close the grill lid. Once hot, add the beef in a single layer. Close the grill lid and cook, turning every 5 to 6 minutes, for 20 to 24 minutes total or until browned on all sides. Transfer to a plate.
5. Add the onion, carrots, celery, and garlic to the Dutch oven and stir to combine. Close the grill lid and cook, stirring occasionally, for 8 to 10 minutes or until softened and browned. Season with salt and pepper.
6. Stir in the tomato paste. Close the grill lid and cook for 1 minute or until bright red.
7. Pour in the broth to deglaze: Bring to a boil, and gently scrape the bottom of the Dutch oven with a wooden spoon to loosen any browned bits.

8. Add the bay leaves, potatoes, and beef. Cover the Dutch oven with a tight-fitting lid. Remove from the heat.
9. Wearing barbecue gloves, carefully remove the grate, install the heat deflector, and replace the grate. Reduce the grill temperature to 350°F.
10. Put the Dutch oven back on the grate. Close the grill lid and cook for 1 hour 30 minutes to 1 hour 45 minutes or until the beef is tender. Discard the bay leaves. Serve immediately.

Grill-Braised Coq Au Vin

Serves 4 to 6

Ingredients:

- 1 large Vidalia onion, cut into 8 wedges
- 8 cloves garlic, peeled
- 1 (2-ounce) can oil-packed anchovy fillets, drained
- 3/4 cup fresh flat-leaf parsley leaves
- 1/4 cup fresh rosemary leaves
- 1 teaspoon kosher salt
- 1/2 teaspoon freshly ground black pepper
- 2 chickens (about 3 pounds each), cut into quarters
- 1 (750-ml) bottle dry, fruity red wine
- Olive oil
- 8 ounces cremini mushrooms, trimmed and sliced

Method:

1. Place the onion, garlic, anchovy fillets, parsley, rosemary, salt, and pepper in a food processor and pulse until the onion is finely chopped.
2. Take the chicken quarters and place in a 2-gallon zip-top plastic bag. Scrape the onion paste into the bag and add the wine. Squish the marinade around the chicken so that all the pieces are well coated and the wine and solids have blended. Press the air out of the bag and seal. Place in a bowl and refrigerate overnight, turning the bag a few times. Don't panic when the chicken turns red. It's from the wine.
3. Light a fire in the kamado grill using your favorite method. After about 10 minutes, place the grill rack in position, close the dome, and open the upper and lower dampers all the way. When the temperature reaches 375°F, adjust the dampers to maintain the temperature.
4. Remove the chicken from the marinade and pat it dry with paper towels. Pour the marinade into a large cast-iron Dutch oven. Brush the chicken lightly with olive oil

and season with salt and pepper. Place on the grill, close the dome, and sear until lightly browned, 3 to 4 minutes per side. Place the chicken and mushrooms in the Dutch oven, cover, place on the grill grate, and close the dome. Braise for about 1½ hours. The breast quarters should have an internal temperature of about 165°F and the thigh quarters about 170°F; the juices should run clear between the thigh and drumstick.

5. Transfer the chicken and mushrooms to a platter and pour the braising liquid over the top. Serve hot or at room temperature.

Frogmore Stew For A Party

Serves 8 to 10

Ingredients:

- 4 tablespoons Chesapeake Bay-style seasoning or crab boil seasoning
- 2 pounds smoked sausage, cut into 2-inch pieces
- 4 sweet onions, peeled, root ends maintained, then cut into quarters
- 12 ears corn, shucked, silks removed, and broken in half
- 4 pounds 3¼-count shrimp
- 8 stone crab claws (optional)
- Cocktail sauce
- Melted unsalted butter
- Grainy mustard

Method:

1. Take a 6- to 8-quart stockpot and fill two-thirds full of water. Add 3 tablespoons of the seasoning and stir to mix.
2. Light a fire in the kamado grill using your favorite method. After about 10 minutes, place the grill rack in position, close the dome, and open the upper and lower dampers all the way. When the temperature reaches 400°F, adjust the dampers to maintain the temperature.
3. Place the pot on the grill and close the dome. Let the water come to a boil (this will take about 15 minutes). Add the sausage and onions, close the dome, and cook for 5 minutes. Add the corn, close the dome, and cook for 2 to 3 minutes. Add the shrimp and crab claws, if using, close the dome, and cook until the shrimp turn pink and have formed a slight "C" shape, about another 5 minutes.
4. Remove the pot from the grill and drain into a colander. Sprinkle the remaining 1 tablespoon seasoning over the "stew." Dump the stew out over a newspaper-lined table. Call everybody to eat, passing the cocktail sauce, butter, and mustard.

Tuscan-Style White Beans

Serves 4

Ingredients:

- 1¼ cups dried cannellini beans, rinsed and picked over
- 1/4 cup extra-virgin olive oil
- 3 garlic cloves, chopped
- 2 medium tomatoes, chopped
- Kosher salt
- Freshly ground black pepper
- 5 cups low-sodium chicken broth
- 1 bunch fresh sage
- 1 bay leaf

Method:

1. In a large bowl, cover the beans with water by 2 inches; soak overnight, then drain.
2. Bring the grill to 400°F with the cooking grate and heat deflector installed, then preheat a 5- quart cast iron Dutch oven on the grate with the grill lid closed.
3. Pour the oil into the Dutch oven and close the grill lid. Once hot, add the garlic. Close the grill lid and cook for 30 seconds to 1 minute or until golden brown.
4. Add the tomatoes. Close the grill lid and cook for 2 to 3 minutes or until slightly softened. Season with salt and pepper.
5. Add the beans, broth, sage, and bay leaf. Cover the Dutch oven with a tight-fitting lid. Close the grill lid and cook for 1 hour 30 minutes to 1 hour 45 minutes or until the beans are tender. Season with salt and pepper. Discard the bay leaves and sage. Serve immediately.

Kashmiri Braised Lamb (Rogan Josh)

Serves 6

Ingredients:

- 2 pounds bone-in lamb shanks
- Kosher salt
- 1 tablespoon ghee or unsalted butter
- 1 medium red onion, coarsely chopped
- 4 garlic cloves, finely chopped
- 1 (1-inch) piece fresh ginger, peeled and finely chopped
- 2 tablespoons tomato paste
- 4 bay leaves
- 2 teaspoons ground coriander
- 1½ teaspoons ground cardamom
- 1 teaspoon ground cinnamon
- 1 teaspoon ground turmeric
- 10 cloves
- 5 dried red chiles, such as chile de árbol
- 2¾ cups water
- 1/2 cup greek yogurt

Method:

1. Season the lamb generously with salt. Refrigerate overnight.
2. Pat the lamb dry.
3. Bring the grill to 500°F with the cooking grate installed, then preheat a 5-quart cast iron Dutch oven on the grate with the grill lid closed.
4. Put the ghee in the Dutch oven and close the grill lid. Once hot, add the lamb in a single layer. Close the grill lid and cook, turning halfway through, for 10 to 12 minutes total or until browned on both sides. Transfer to a plate.
5. Add the onion to the Dutch oven. Close the grill lid and cook, stirring occasionally, for 2 to 3 minutes or until starting to soften. Season with salt.

6. Add the garlic and ginger. Close the grill lid and cook, stirring frequently, for 30 to 60 seconds or until fragrant.
7. Add the tomato paste, bay leaves, coriander, cardamom, cinnamon, turmeric, cloves, and chiles and stir to combine. Cook, stirring, for 1 to 2 minutes or until the tomato paste turns bright red. Season with salt.
8. Add the lamb; turn to coat with the tomato-spice mixture. Add the water. Cover the Dutch oven with a tight-fitting lid. Remove from the heat.
9. Wearing barbecue gloves, carefully remove the grate, install the heat deflector, and replace the grate. Reduce the grill temperature to 350°F.
10. Put the Dutch oven back on the grate. Close the grill lid and cook for 55 minutes to 1 hour 5 minutes or until the lamb is tender.
11. Stir in the yogurt. Cook for 5 minutes or until the flavors meld. Serve immediately.

Burgoo

Serves 8

Ingredients:

- 3 bacon slices
- 2 large onions, diced
- 8 tablespoons (1 stick) unsalted butter
- 1 pound bone-in beef shank
- 1 pound boneless, skinless chicken thighs, diced
- 1 (28-ounce) can crushed tomatoes
- 1 pound yukon gold potatoes, cut into 1-inch dice
- 1 cup corn kernels
- 1 gallon water
- 1 tablespoon kosher salt
- 1 tablespoon freshly ground black pepper

Method:

1. Bring the grill to 500°F with the cooking grate installed, then preheat a 5-quart cast iron Dutch oven on the grate with the grill lid closed.
2. Put the bacon in the Dutch oven. Close the grill lid and cook for 1 to 2 minutes or until browned and crispy around the edges. Transfer to a plate. Once cool enough to handle, crumble.
3. Add the onions and stir to coat with bacon fat. Close the grill lid and cook for 8 to 10 minutes or until slightly softened and browned.
4. Add the butter, beef, chicken, tomatoes, potatoes, corn, water, bacon, salt, and pepper. Close the grill lid and bring to a boil, then remove from the heat.
5. Wearing barbecue gloves, carefully remove the grate, install the heat deflector, and replace the grate. Reduce the grill temperature to 350°F.
6. Put the Dutch oven back on the grate. Close the grill lid and simmer for 3 hours 30 minutes or until the beef separates easily from the bone and is tender; check on the burgoo's consistency during the last hour of cooking, stirring frequently. Serve immediately.

Coq Au Vin

Serves 4

Ingredients:

- 1 (4- to 5-pound) whole chicken, quartered
- Kosher salt
- 3 bacon slices
- 4 ounces pearl onions
- 7 ounces white or cremini mushrooms, sliced
- 2 tablespoons unsalted butter
- 1 medium onion, coarsely chopped
- 3 medium carrots, coarsely chopped
- 3 garlic cloves, coarsely chopped
- Freshly ground black pepper
- 3 cups red wine
- 2 cups low-sodium chicken broth
- 10 fresh thyme sprigs
- 2 bay leaves

Method:

1. Season the chicken generously with salt. Refrigerate overnight.
2. Pat the chicken dry.
3. Bring the grill to 500°F with the cooking grate installed, then preheat a 5-quart cast iron Dutch oven on the grate with the grill lid closed.
4. Put the bacon in the Dutch oven. Close the grill lid and cook for 1 to 2 minutes or until browned and crispy around the edges. Transfer to a plate. Once cool enough to handle, crumble.
5. In two batches, add the chicken to the Dutch oven, skin-side down and in a single layer. Close the grill lid and cook for 8 to 10 minutes or until the skin is browned. Transfer to a plate.

6. Meanwhile, put the pearl onions in a small saucepan with just enough water to cover. Bring to a boil over high heat on the stove top. Cook for 1 minute. Drain and rinse with cool water; peel.
7. Add the mushrooms to the Dutch oven. Close the grill lid and cook, stirring once, 7 to 9 minutes or until browned. Season with salt. Using a slotted spoon, transfer to a plate.
8. Add the butter to the Dutch oven and close the grill lid. When melted, add the chopped onion, pearl onions, carrots, and garlic. Close the grill lid and cook, stirring occasionally, for 8 to 10 minutes or until softened and browned. Season with salt and pepper.
9. Pour in the wine and broth to deglaze: Close the grill lid, bring to a boil, then gently scrape the bottom of the Dutch oven with a wooden spoon to loosen any browned bits.
10. Add the thyme and bay leaves, close the grill lid, and cook for 21 to 25 minutes or until reduced by half. Season with salt and pepper. Add the chicken and bacon. Cover the Dutch oven with a tight-fitting lid. Remove from the heat.
11. Wearing barbecue gloves, carefully remove the grate, install the heat deflector, and replace the grate. Reduce the grill temperature to 350°F.
12. Put the Dutch oven back on the grate. Close the grill lid and cook for 45 minutes to 1 hour or until the chicken is tender.
13. Discard the thyme and bay leaves. Stir in the mushrooms and let sit for 10 minutes before serving.

Lobio

Serves 4

Ingredients:

- 1¼ cups dried red kidney beans, rinsed and picked over
- 1 tablespoon extra-virgin olive oil
- 1 medium red onion, finely diced
- 3 garlic cloves, chopped
- 2 teaspoons ground coriander
- 1/4 teaspoon cayenne pepper
- 5½ cups low-sodium chicken broth
- 2 bay leaves
- Kosher salt
- Freshly ground black pepper
- 1 cup walnuts, toasted and ground
- 1/2 cup chopped fresh cilantro

Method:

1. In a large bowl, cover the beans with water by 2 inches; soak overnight, then drain.
2. Bring the grill to 400°F with the cooking grate and heat deflector installed, then preheat a 5-quart cast iron Dutch oven with the grill lid closed.
3. Pour the oil into the Dutch oven and close the grill lid. Once hot, add the onion and garlic. Close the grill lid and cook for 8 to 10 minutes or until softened and browned.
4. Stir in the coriander and cayenne. Close the grill lid and cook for 1 minute or until the flavors meld.
5. Add the beans, broth, and bay leaves. Cover the Dutch oven with a tight-fitting lid. Close the grill lid and cook for 1 hour 30 minutes to 1 hour 45 minutes or until the beans are tender.
6. Season with salt and pepper. Stir in the ground walnuts, and sprinkle with the cilantro. Serve immediately.

Chapter 5: Baking

Kamado S'Mores

Serves 6 to 8

Ingredients:

- 12 ounces semisweet baking chocolate, coarsely chopped
- 4 cups miniature marshmallows
- Graham crackers

Method:

1. Light a fire in the kamado grill using your favorite method. After about 10 minutes, place the grill rack in position, close the dome, and open the upper and lower dampers all the way. When the temperature reaches 450°F, adjust the dampers to maintain the temperature.
2. Sprinkle the chocolate evenly in the bottom of a 10-inch cast-iron skillet. Cover the chocolate with the marshmallows. Place the skillet on the grill, close the dome, and bake until the marshmallows are browned, about 5 minutes.
3. Remove the skillet from the kamado and let stand for 5 minutes. Serve with the graham crackers, using them to dip into the skillet.

Sweet Potato Biscuits with Orange-Honey Butter

Serves 10 to 12

Ingredients:

- 1 cup self-rising soft wheat flour
- 1 tablespoon firmly packed light brown sugar
- 1/2 teaspoon baking powder
- 1/8 teaspoon ground cinnamon
- 1/4 cup (1/2 stick) cold unsalted butter
- 1 large sweet potato, baked until tender and flesh removed from skin, or 1 (15.5-ounce) can sweet potatoes, drained and mashed
- 1/2 cup (1 stick) unsalted butter, softened
- 1 tablespoons honey
- Grated zest of 1 orange

Method:

1. Light a fire in the kamado grill using your favorite method. After about 10 minutes, place the grill rack in position, close the dome, and open the upper and lower dampers all the way. When the temperature reaches 500°F, adjust the dampers to maintain the temperature.
2. While the grill comes to temperature, in a large bowl, combine the flour, brown sugar, baking powder, and cinnamon. Cut the cold butter into pieces and scatter on top of the flour. Work the butter into the flour with a pastry cutter, two knives, or your fingertips if you have cold hands until the mixture resemble large peas. Stir at least 3/4 cup of the sweet potato into the flour until a dough forms. Lightly flour a work surface and knead the dough 2 or 3 times.
3. Put a silicone baking mat or sheet of parchment paper on a flameproof baking sheet. Pat the dough until it is 1/2 inch thick. Flour a 2-inch biscuit cutter and cut out as many biscuits as possible, placing them on the baking sheet with their sides touching. Pat the scraps together and cut out more biscuits.
4. Place the baking sheet on the grill, close the dome, and bake until the tops are brown, 10 to 12 minutes.

5. While the biscuits are baking, cream the softened butter, honey, and orange zest together.
6. Transfer the biscuits to a plate and serve hot or at room temperature with the orange-honey butter.

Proper Cornbread

Serves 8

Ingredients:

- 2 cups self-rising cornmeal mix
- 1⅓ cups buttermilk
- 1/4 cup corn oil
- 1 large egg, slightly beaten
- 1 to 2 tablespoons sugar if you were born north of the Mason-Dixon line

Method:

1. Spray an 8- or 10-inch cast-iron skillet or an 8inch square flameproof baking pan with 2-inch sides with cooking spray.
2. Light a fire in the kamado grill using your favorite method. After about 10 minutes, place the grill rack in position, close the dome, and open the upper and lower dampers all the way. When the temperature reaches 375°F, adjust the dampers to maintain the temperature. Place the prepared pan on the grill and close the dome.
3. In a large bowl, whisk the cornmeal mix, buttermilk, oil, egg, and sugar, if using, together.
4. Pour the batter into the heated skillet. Close the dome and bake until the cornbread pulls away from the side of the pan and a toothpick inserted in the center comes out clean, 20 to 25 minutes for a 10-inch skillet or 25 to 30 minutes for an 8-inch skillet or pan.
5. Remove the skillet from the oven, cut the cornbread into 8 wedges or squares, and serve hot.

Country Sausage-Laced Baked Beans

Serves 8 to 10 or more

Ingredients:

- 3 (32-ounce) cans pork and beans, drained
- 2 pounds country breakfast sausage, browned and crumbled
- 2 medium onions, thinly sliced into half moons
- 1 cup firmly packed light brown sugar
- 1 cup dark corn syrup
- 1/4 cup prepared yellow mustard
- 1 tablespoon dry mustard
- 2 teaspoons Worcestershire sauce

Method:

1. Light a fire in the kamado grill using your favorite method. After about 10 minutes, place the grill rack in position, close the dome, and open the upper and lower dampers all the way. When the temperature reaches 350°F, adjust the dampers to maintain the temperature.
2. Pour the drained pork and beans in a 9- x 13-inch disposable aluminum-foil baking pan or a cast-iron Dutch oven. Add the sausage and onions and stir to mix. Add the remaining ingredients and stir to blend well.
3. Set the baking pan on the grill, close the dome, and bake for at least 1 hour; 1½ hours is better. Cooking the beans the day before and reheating them for about 30 minutes in a preheated 350°F oven will get you the very best flavor.

Sweet Potato Pie

Serves 8

Ingredients:

- 2 pounds sweet potatoes, peeled and cut into 1-inch slices
- 1 tablespoon vegetable oil
- 8 tablespoons (1 stick) unsalted butter, at room temperature
- 3 large eggs, beaten
- 1 cup whole milk
- 1 tablespoon kosher salt
- 1 teaspoon freshly ground black pepper
- 1 (9-inch) refrigerated pie shell

Method:

1. Bring the grill to 500°F with the cooking grate and heat deflector installed.
2. In a large bowl, toss the sweet potatoes with the oil.
3. Put the sweet potatoes on the grate. Close the lid and cook for 25 minutes or until fork-tender and golden brown around the edges. Transfer to a bowl.
4. Add the butter. Mash until smooth.
5. Stir in the eggs and then the milk until fully incorporated. Add the salt and pepper and stir to combine. Pour the filling into the pie shell.
6. Reduce the grill temperature to 375°F. Put the pie on the grate. Close the lid and cook for 1 hour or until a knife inserted into the center comes out clean.
7. Put on a wire rack to cool completely before serving.

Cornbread

Serves 6

Ingredients:

- Unsalted butter, at room temperature, for coating the skillet
- 1½ cups finely ground white cornmeal
- 1½ teaspoons baking powder
- 1 teaspoon kosher salt
- 1¾ cups milk
- 1 large egg, beaten

Method:

1. Bring the grill to 375°F with the cooking grate and heat deflector installed. Butter the bottom and sides of a 10-inch cast iron skillet.
2. In a medium bowl, mix together the cornmeal, baking powder, and salt.
3. Stir in the milk, then the egg. Pour the batter into the skillet.
4. Put the skillet on the grate. Close the lid and cook for 30 minutes or until golden brown on top and a tester inserted in the center comes out clean.
5. Serve immediately.

Molasses Cake

Serves 8

Ingredients:

- 2/3 cup unsalted butter, plus more for the pan, at room temperature
- 1½ cups all-purpose flour
- 1½ teaspoons baking powder
- 1 teaspoon kosher salt
- 1 cup unsulfured blackstrap molasses
- 1/2 cup whole milk
- 1 large egg

Method:

1. Bring the grill to 375°F with the cooking grate and heat deflector installed. Butter the bottom and sides of a 10-inch cast iron skillet.
2. In a medium bowl, mix together the flour, baking powder, and salt.
3. In the bowl of an electric mixer, cream together the butter, molasses, milk, and egg on medium speed for 3 minutes.
4. Reduce the speed to low. Add the flour mixture, scraping down the side of the bowl as needed, until fully incorporated. Transfer to the skillet.
5. Put the skillet on the grate. Close the lid and cook for 30 minutes or until a knife inserted into the center comes out clean.
6. Put on a wire rack to cool completely before serving.

Savory Baked Apples

Serves 8

Ingredients:

- 1/2 cup finely chopped onion
- 1 tablespoon unsalted butter
- 1/2 pound country breakfast sausage
- 1/2 teaspoon ground cinnamon
- 1/4 teaspoon ground allspice
- 1/4 teaspoon ground ginger
- 1/4 teaspoon kosher salt
- 9 medium Granny Smith apples
- 1 cup chopped pecans
- 2 cups apple cider, warmed

Method:

1. Place a medium skillet over medium heat and add the onion and butter. Cook until the onion is soft, about 5 minutes, stirring a few times. Add the sausage, using a spatula to break it apart into chunks. Sprinkle the spices and salt over the sausage and cook until the sausage is no longer pink, about 12 minutes.
2. Peel and core one of the apples and cut into small chunks. Add to the sausage and cook for a couple of minutes. Stir in the pecans. Remove from the heat and let cool.
3. Core the remaining apples and stuff with the sausage mixture. Place the stuffed apples in a shallow flameproof baking pan and pour the warm cider around them.
4. Light a fire in the kamado grill using your favorite method. After about 10 minutes, place the grill rack in position, close the dome, and open the upper and lower dampers all the way. When the temperature reaches 350°F, adjust the dampers to maintain the temperature.
5. Place the baking pan on the grill and close the dome. Bake until the apples still hold their shape but can be easily pierced with a knife, about 40 minutes. Serve warm or at room temperature.

Pumpkin Pie

Serves 8

Ingredients:

- 1 (15-ounce) can pure pumpkin pureee
- 2 large eggs, beaten
- 1/3 cup packed light brown sugar
- 1 tablespoon ground cinnamon
- 2 teaspoons ground allspice
- 1/2 teaspoon ground cloves
- 1 (9-inch) graham cracker pie shell

Method:

1. Bring the grill to 350°F with the cooking grate and heat deflector installed.
2. In a large bowl, whisk together the pumpkin purée, eggs, sugar, cinnamon, allspice, and cloves until smooth and thoroughly combined. Pour into the pie shell.
3. Put the pie on the grate. Close the lid and cook for 40 to 50 minutes or until the filling is set.
4. Put on a wire rack to cool completely before serving.

Oatmeal-Berry Crisp

Serves 6 to 8

Ingredients:

- 1½ cups hulled and quartered fresh strawberries
- 1½ cups fresh blueberries
- 1½ cups fresh raspberries
- 1/3 cup granulated sugar
- 2 cups all-purpose flour
- 2 cups rolled (old-fashioned) oats
- 1½ cups firmly packed light brown sugar
- 1 teaspoon ground cinnamon
- 1/2 teaspoon ground nutmeg
- 3/4 cup (1½ sticks) cold unsalted butter
- Ice cream (optional)

Method:

1. At least 2 hours before you plan to bake the crisp, toss the fruit and granulated sugar together in a large bowl. Set aside at room temperature, tossing the mixture together occasionally.
2. Light a fire in the kamado grill using your favorite method. After about 10 minutes, place the grill rack in position, close the dome, and open the upper and lower dampers all the way. When the temperature reaches 350°F, adjust the dampers to maintain the temperature.
3. While the grill comes to temperature, combine the flour, oats, brown sugar, cinnamon, and nutmeg in another large bowl. Work the butter into the mixture, using a pastry cutter, two knives, or your fingertips, until it has the texture of small peas. Press half the mixture into the bottom of a 9- x 13-inch cast-iron or other flameproof baking pan. Pour in the berries with their juice. Sprinkle the remaining crumble mixture over the top of the berries.

4. Place the baking pan on the grill, close the dome, and bake until the fruit is bubbly and the topping is golden brown, 30 to 40 minutes. Serve warm with ice cream, if desired.

Meatballs In Tomato Sauce

Serves 4

Ingredients:

- 1½ pounds ground beef
- 1 large egg
- 4 garlic cloves, finely chopped
- 3/4 cup finely diced red onion
- 1/2 cup plain bread crumbs
- 1 tablespoon dried oregano kosher salt
- Freshly ground black pepper
- 1 teaspoon olive oil
- 3½ cups tomato sauce
- 1/2 cup grated parmesan cheese

Method:

1. Bring the grill to 350°F with the cooking grate and heat deflector installed, then preheat a 5-quart cast iron Dutch oven on the grate with the grill lid closed.
2. Meanwhile, in a large bowl, gently combine the ground beef, egg, garlic, onion, bread crumbs, and oregano. Season generously with salt and pepper. Mix until just incorporated; form into 1-inch meatballs.
3. Pour the oil into the Dutch oven and close the grill lid. Once hot, and working in batches if necessary, add the meatballs in a single layer. Close the grill lid and cook, turning occasionally, for 16 to 20 minutes total or until lightly browned on all sides.
4. Add the tomato sauce. Cover the Dutch oven with a tight-fitting lid. Close the grill lid and cook for 10 minutes or until the flavors meld.
5. Remove from the heat, sprinkle with the Parmesan, and serve immediately.

Twice-Baked Potatoes

Serves 6

Ingredients:

- 3 large russet potatoes
- 1/4 cup extra-virgin olive oil
- Kosher salt
- 3/4 cup heavy cream
- 1/2 cup chopped green onions
- 3 tablespoons unsalted butter
- 1½ cups grated Gruyère or smoked Gouda cheese (about 6 ounces)
- Freshly ground black pepper

Method:

1. Light a fire in the kamado grill using your favorite method. After about 10 minutes, place the grill rack in position, close the dome, and open the upper and lower dampers all the way. When the temperature reaches 450°F, adjust the dampers to maintain the temperature.
2. Brush the potatoes all over with the oil. Pierce them with the tines of a fork and sprinkle with salt. Wrap each potato in aluminum foil and place on the grill. Close the dome and cook until the potatoes are soft and easily pierced with a knife, about 1 hour.
3. Remove the potatoes from the grill and let rest for about 15 minutes. Heat the cream in a small saucepan until hot (but not boiling) and throw in the green onions. Remove from the heat.
4. Unwrap the potatoes, cut each one in half lengthwise, and scoop out the flesh. Be careful not to tear the skin. Place the potato flesh in a large bowl and add the butter and 1 cup of the cheese. Pour in the hot cream; using a sturdy fork, mix together until the mixture is smooth and the cheese is melted. Season with salt and pepper, then spoon the mixture into each of the potato-skin shells. Sprinkle the tops evenly with the remaining 1/2 cup cheese.

5. Put the potatoes in a flameproof baking pan and place on the grill. Close the dome and heat until the cheese is melted, about 5 minutes. Serve immediately.

Jerk-Marinated Tofu

Serves 2

Ingredients:

- 1 (12-ounce) block extra-firm tofu
- 1/3 cup jerk marinade
- 2 tablespoons soy sauce

Method:

1. Press the tofu for 30 minutes using a heavy weight (such as a cast iron skillet). Pat dry and transfer to a shallow dish. Pour in the marinade and turn the tofu over to coat; marinate for 30 minutes at room temperature.
2. Bring the grill to 400°F with the cooking grate and heat deflector installed.
3. Put the tofu on the grate. Close the lid and cook for 15 to 20 minutes or until the marinade has caramelized around the edges and the tofu is heated through. Transfer to a plate.
4. Cut into 1/4-inch-thick slices, drizzle with the soy sauce, and serve immediately.

Shakshouka

Serves 4

Ingredients:

- 1 tablespoon extra-virgin olive oil
- 1 medium onion, chopped
- 3 garlic cloves, chopped
- 2 medium bell peppers, seeded and chopped
- 1 large tomato, chopped
- 2 teaspoons cumin seeds
- 1 teaspoon ground coriander
- 1/2 teaspoon cayenne pepper
- Kosher salt
- Freshly ground black pepper
- 1 (15-ounce) can diced tomatoes
- 4 large eggs
- 1/2 cup crumbled feta cheese (optional)
- 1/4 cup chopped fresh mint or flat-leaf parsley

Method:

1. Bring the grill to 400°F with the cooking grate and heat deflector installed, then preheat a 10-inch cast iron skillet on the grate with the grill lid closed.
2. Pour the oil into the skillet and close the grill lid. Once hot, add the onion, garlic, peppers, chopped tomato, cumin seeds, coriander, and cayenne. Season with salt and pepper and stir to combine. Close the lid and cook, stirring once or twice, for 24 to 28 minutes or until softened.
3. Stir in the diced tomatoes with their juice. Close the lid and cook for 9 to 12 minutes or until thickened slightly.
4. Form four wells in the sauce and add one egg to each well. Close the lid and cook for 4 to 6 minutes or until the whites have set but the yolks are still runny.
5. Remove from the heat, sprinkle with the feta (if using) and mint, and serve immediately.

Mediterranean Baked Fish

Serves 4

Ingredients:

- 6 plum tomatoes, roughly chopped
- 1 cup pitted Kalamata olives
- 1/2 cup thinly sliced fennel bulb
- 4 cloves garlic, run through a press
- 1 shallot, finely chopped
- 1 teaspoon Creole seasoning
- 1 teaspoon dried herbes de Provence
- 4 (6-ounce) tilapia or other sturdy white fish fillets

Method:

1. Place the tomatoes, olives, fennel, garlic, and shallot in a 9- x 13-inch baking pan or disposable aluminum-foil pan or cast-iron skillet.
2. In a small bowl, combine the Creole seasoning and herbes de Provence. Sprinkle this mixture over the fish fillets, coating them well on both sides. Nestle the fish fillets in among the vegetables in the pan.
3. Light a fire in the kamado grill using your favorite method. After about 10 minutes, place the grill rack in position, close the dome, and open the upper and lower dampers all the way. When the temperature reaches 350°F, adjust the dampers to maintain the temperature.
4. Place the baking dish on the grill, close the dome, and bake until the tip of a cake tester inserted into the center of one of the fillets is just warm to your lip, about 20 minutes.
5. Transfer the fish to a platter and cover with the tomato mixture and all the juices that have accumulated in the pan. Serve immediately.

Dirty Rice

Serves 8

Ingredients:

- 1 pound smoked sausage, such as andouille, removed from the casing and crumbled
- 8 ounces chicken livers, trimmed of membranes
- 2 tablespoons unsalted butter
- 2 cups finely diced red onion
- 1 cup finely diced celery
- 1 cup finely diced green bell pepper
- 6 garlic cloves, chopped
- 3 cups cooked white rice
- 1¼ cups low-sodium chicken broth
- 1 tablespoon kosher salt
- 1 tablespoon sweet paprika
- 2 teaspoons cayenne pepper
- 1 teaspoon freshly ground black pepper
- 1 teaspoon dried oregano
- 1/2 teaspoon ground cinnamon

Method:

1. Bring the grill to 500°F with the cooking grate installed, then preheat a 5-quart cast iron Dutch oven on the grate with the grill lid closed.
2. Put the sausage and chicken livers in the Dutch oven. Close the grill lid and cook, stirring once, for 7 to 8 minutes or until browned. Using a slotted spoon, transfer to a cutting board. Once cool enough to handle, finely chop.
3. Add the butter, onion, celery, bell pepper, and garlic to the Dutch oven. Close the grill lid and cook, stirring occasionally, for 6 to 7 minutes or until slightly softened. Remove from the heat.
4. Wearing barbecue gloves, carefully remove the grate, install the heat deflector, and replace the grate. Reduce the grill temperature to 400°F.

5. Put the Dutch oven back on the grate. Add the cooked rice, broth, sausage and chicken liver mixture, salt, paprika, cayenne, pepper, oregano, and cinnamon to the Dutch oven and stir to combine. Close the grill lid and bring to a simmer. Cook for 4 to 6 minutes or until the liquid and seasonings are absorbed. Serve immediately.

Biscuit Breakfast Pudding

Serves 6 to 8

Ingredients:

- 20 to 24 baked tea biscuits or 8 baked regular biscuits (baked frozen biscuits are okay)
- 1 pound mild or hot country breakfast sausage
- 3 tablespoons all-purpose flour
- 2 cups whole milk
- Freshly ground black pepper
- 6 large eggs, beaten
- 1 cup shredded cheese (I like a mixture of cheddar and Gruyère)
- Maple syrup for serving

Method:

1. Line the bottom of a 15-inch cast-iron baking pan or skillet with the biscuits. You should have some left to crumble on top.
2. In a large skillet over medium heat, brown the sausage, using a spatula to break apart large chunks. This will take 8 to 10 minutes. Once all the pink is gone, sprinkle in the flour and stir to coat the sausage. Continue to cook for another 1 to 2 minutes. Slowly start stirring in the milk. You may not need the entire 2 cups. You want the gravy to build and thicken but not be too thick; this usually takes about 5 minutes. Season to taste with pepper. Spoon the gravy evenly over the biscuits. Use all the gravy. Pour the beaten eggs over the top. Crumble the remaining biscuits over the eggs. Scatter the cheese evenly over everything.
3. Light a fire in the kamado grill using your favorite method. After about 10 minutes, place the grill rack in position, close the dome, and open the upper and lower dampers all the way. When the temperature reaches 350°F, adjust the dampers to maintain the temperature.
4. Place the baking pan on the grill, close the dome, and bake until the cheese has browned a bit and the center of the pudding feels a little firm to the touch, but is still slightly liquid, 20 to 25 minutes.

5. Remove the pan from the grill and let sit 10 minutes. Cut into serving pieces and drizzle with maple syrup if desired. Serve immediately.

Pancetta Frittata

Serves 4 to 6

Ingredients:

- 8 large eggs
- 2 tablespoons milk
- 1 cup shredded fontina cheese
- Kosher salt and freshly ground black pepper
- 1 tablespoon unsalted butter
- 1/2 cup diced onion
- 4 ounces pancetta, diced
- 1/4 cup sour cream for serving (optional)

Method:

1. Light a fire in the kamado grill using your favorite method. After about 10 minutes, place the grill rack in position, close the dome, and open the upper and lower dampers all the way. When the temperature reaches 400°F, adjust the dampers to maintain the temperature.
2. In a large bowl, whisk the eggs, milk, cheese, and salt and pepper to taste together.
3. In a 12-inch cast-iron skillet over medium heat, melt the butter; when it foams, add the onion and cook until it is soft and some color develops, about 10 minutes, stirring occasionally. Add the pancetta and cook, stirring a few times, until it takes on a little color, about 5 minutes. Pour the egg mixture into the pan and stir it around with a spatula so that the eggs make full contact with the bottom of the pan.
4. Immediately, take the pan and place it on the grill. Close the dome and bake until the frittata is puffed up and golden brown, 20 to 25 minutes.
5. Remove the skillet from the grill and let cool for about 10 minutes. Slice the frittata into wedges and serve with sour cream, if desired.

BEC PizZa

Serves 2

Ingredients:

- 1 (11-ounce) can refrigerated thin-crust pizza dough
- All-purpose flour, for dusting
- 8 ounces fresh mozzarella, torn into small pieces
- 1½ ounces goat cheese, crumbled
- 4 bacon slices
- 4 large eggs

Method:

1. Bring the grill to 650°F with the cooking grate and heat deflector installed, then preheat a pizza stone on the grate with the lid closed.
2. On a lightly floured work surface, roll out the dough to a 12- to 13-inch diameter.
3. Top with the mozzarella and goat cheeses and the bacon.
4. Put the pizza on parchment paper on the stone and crack the eggs on top. Close the lid and cook for 1 to 2 minutes or until the cheese is melted, the egg whites are set but the yolks are still runny, and the bacon is cooked. Serve immediately.

Molasses Baked Beans

Serves 8

Ingredients:

- 2½ cups dried navy beans, rinsed and picked over
- 3 bacon slices
- 1 tablespoon tomato paste
- 3 cups low-sodium beef broth
- 1/2 cup canned diced tomatoes
- 1/4 cup unsulfured blackstrap molasses
- 1/4 cup packed light brown sugar
- 2 tablespoons yellow mustard
- 2 tablespoons kosher salt

Method:

1. In a large bowl, cover the beans with water by 2 inches; soak overnight.
2. The next day, drain the beans, transfer them to a 5-quart cast iron Dutch oven, and cover again with water by 2 inches.
3. Bring to a boil on the stove top, reduce the heat to a simmer, and cook for 30 to 35 minutes, or until tender, and drain. Dry the inside of the Dutch oven.
4. Bring the grill to 500°F with the cooking grate installed, then preheat the Dutch oven on the grate with the grill lid closed.
5. Put the bacon in the Dutch oven. Close the grill lid and cook for 1 to 2 minutes or until browned and crispy around the edges. Transfer to a plate. Once cool enough to handle, crumble.
6. Stir the tomato paste into the bacon fat. Close the grill lid and cook for 1 minute or until bright red. Remove from the heat.
7. Wearing barbecue gloves, carefully remove the grate, install the heat deflector, and replace the grate. Reduce the grill temperature to 350°F.
8. Add the broth, tomatoes (with their juice), molasses, sugar, mustard, salt, and bacon to the Dutch oven and stir to combine. Cover the Dutch oven with a tight-

fitting lid. Put back on the grate. Close the grill lid and cook for 1 hour 10 minutes to 1 hour 20 minutes or until thickened. Serve immediately.

Chapter 6: Rubs, Sauces and more

Middle Eastern Za'tar Seasoning

Makes about 1/4 cup

Ingredients:

- 3 tablespoons dried thyme
- 2 teaspoons ground sumac
- 1/2 teaspoon kosher salt or to taste
- 1 tablespoon toasted sesame seeds

Method:

1. Using a mortar and pestle, grind together the thyme, sumac, and salt until pulverized. Add the sesame seeds and taste for seasoning. Store in an airtight container in a cool, dry place.

Tandoori Seasoning

Makes about 1/4 cup

Ingredients:

- 3 tablespoons curry powder
- 1 teaspoon hot paprika
- 1 teaspoon sweet paprika
- 1 teaspoon ground cumin
- 1 teaspoon ground turmeric
- 1 teaspoon ground coriander
- 1/2 teaspoon freshly grated nutmeg
- 1/2 teaspoon ground ginger
- 1/2 teaspoon ground cardamom

Method:

1. Combine all the ingredients and store in an airtight container in a cool, dry place.

Aioli

Makes 1¼ cups

Ingredients:

- 1 large egg
- 1 cup vegetable oil
- 2 garlic cloves, peeled
- 1/2 teaspoon kosher salt

Method:

1. Put the egg in the bowl of a small food processor. Blend until beaten.
2. With the machine running, slowly stream in the oil through the feed tube until emulsified (the mixture thickens).
3. Blend in the garlic and salt.
4. Transfer to an airtight container, refrigerate, and use within 5 days.

Lemon-Herb Marinade

Makes about 1 cup

Ingredients:

- 1/2 cup extra-virgin olive oil
- 1/4 cup chopped fresh rosemary
- 1/4 cup chopped fresh thyme
- 1/4 cup chopped fresh basil
- 1¼ teaspoons kosher salt
- 1 teaspoon freshly ground black pepper
- 4 cloves garlic, minced
- Grated zest and juice of 2 lemons

Method:

1. In a small bowl, whisk all the ingredients together. For poultry or meat, use it to marinate for up to 2 days; for fish, no more than 2 hours.

Jerk Marinade

Makes 1¼ cups

Ingredients:

- 5 habanero peppers, stemmed
- 3 garlic cloves, peeled
- 1 small red onion, coarsely chopped
- 1 tablespoon ground allspice
- 1 teaspoon ground cinnamon
- 1/2 teaspoon ground cloves
- 10 fresh thyme sprigs, leaves picked and stems discarded
- 1 tablespoon light brown sugar
- Juice of 1 lime
- 3 tablespoons soy sauce
- 2 tablespoons vegetable oil

Method:

1. Put the habanero peppers, garlic, onion, allspice, cinnamon, cloves, thyme, sugar, lime juice, soy sauce, and oil in the bowl of a small food processor. Blend until combined and no large chunks of garlic remain.
2. Transfer to an airtight container and refrigerate up to 1 week.

Nikki's Lamb Marinade

Makes 1¾ cups

Ingredients:

- 3/4 cup vegetable oil
- 1/2 cup red wine vinegar
- 1/2 cup chopped onion
- 2 teaspoons Dijon mustard
- 2 teaspoons kosher salt
- 1/2 teaspoon dried oregano
- 1/2 teaspoon dried basil
- 1/8 teaspoon freshly ground black pepper
- 2 cloves garlic, bruised
- 1 bay leaf

Method:

1. In a medium bowl, whisk all the ingredients together. Use it to marinate your choice of protein at least 24 hours and up to 48 hours.

Memphis-Style Dry Rub

Makes about 1 cup (enough for 10 to 12 pounds of ribs)

Ingredients:

- 1/2 cup kosher salt
- 2 tablespoons freshly ground black pepper
- 2 tablespoons sweet paprika
- 2 tablespoons dried oregano
- 2 teaspoons garlic powder
- 2 teaspoons cayenne pepper

Method:

1. In a small bowl, combine the salt, pepper, paprika, oregano, garlic powder, and cayenne.
2. Transfer to an airtight container, and store for up to 6 months.

Cajun Rub

Makes about 1½ cups

Ingredients:

- 3 tablespoons sweet paprika
- 3 tablespoons kosher salt
- 3 tablespoons freshly ground black pepper
- 3 tablespoons granulated garlic
- 3 tablespoons granulated onion
- 4 teaspoons dried oregano
- 4 teaspoons dried thyme
- 1 tablespoon smoked paprika
- 1 tablespoon cayenne pepper

Method:

1. Combine all the ingredients and store in an airtight container in a cool, dry place. It will keep for several months.

Limeade Pacific Seafood Marinade

Makes about 2 cups

Ingredients:

- 3/4 cup extra-virgin olive oil
- 3/4 cup tamari
- 6 ounces frozen limeade concentrate, thawed
- 2 tablespoons minced garlic
- 2 tablespoons chopped fresh rosemary

Method:

1. In a medium bowl, whisk all the ingredients together.

Japanese Shichimi

Makes about 3 tablespoons

Ingredients:

- 1 tablespoon Szechuan peppercorns
- 1½ teaspoons dried orange peel
- 1 teaspoon black sesame seeds
- 1 teaspoon white sesame seeds
- 1½ teaspoons ground red chile
- 1 teaspoon crushed nori
- 1 teaspoon granulated garlic

Method:

1. Toast the peppercorns in a small skillet over medium heat for 1 minute, then grind into a powder using a mortar and pestle or a coffee or spice grinder. Transfer to a small bowl.
2. Toast the orange peel and sesame seeds in the skillet over medium heat for 1 minute. Add to the peppercorns. Toast the chile for 30 seconds. Add to the peppercorns, along with the nori and garlic. Stir to blend. Store in an airtight container in a cool, dry place.

Kansas City-Style Barbecue Sauce

Makes about 1½ cups

Ingredients:

- 1 cup ketchup
- 1/2 cup apple cider vinegar
- 2 tablespoons worcestershire sauce
- 2 tablespoons unsulfured blackstrap
- Molasses
- 6 tablespoons packed light brown sugar
- 2 tablespoons canola oil
- 6 garlic cloves, finely chopped
- 2 teaspoons kosher salt
- 2 teaspoons sweet paprika
- 1 teaspoon ground cinnamon
- 1 teaspoon cayenne pepper

Method:

1. In a medium bowl, whisk together the ketchup, vinegar, Worcestershire, molasses, and sugar until smooth.
2. In a medium saucepan, heat the oil over medium heat.
3. Add the garlic. Cook for about 30 seconds or until golden.
4. Add the salt, paprika, cinnamon, and cayenne. Cook for 10 seconds or until fragrant.
5. Stir in the ketchup mixture. Bring to a simmer and let simmer for about 1 minute or until the flavors meld.
6. Let cool and refrigerate overnight before using to let the flavors develop.

Peruvian Cilantro Sauce

Makes 1½ cups

Ingredients:

- 1/2 cup aioli
- 3 cups fresh cilantro leaves (from about 3 bunches)
- 2 jalapeno peppers, stemmed and coarsely chopped
- 1/2 teaspoon kosher salt
- 1/4 teaspoon cayenne pepper
- Juice of 2 limes

Method:

1. Put the aioli, cilantro, jalapeño peppers, salt, cayenne, and lime juice in the bowl of a small food processor. Blend until combined.
2. Transfer to an airtight container and refrigerate for up to 5 days.

Canadian-Style Steak Seasoning

Makes about 6 tablespoons

Ingredients:

- 1 tablespoon crushed black peppercorns
- 1 tablespoon sweet paprika
- 1½ teaspoons kosher salt
- 1½ teaspoons granulated garlic
- 1½ teaspoons granulated onion
- 1½ teaspoons ground coriander
- 1½ teaspoons dill seeds, lightly crushed
- 1½ teaspoons crushed red pepper

Method:

1. Combine all the ingredients and store in an airtight container in a cool, dry place.

Best Ever Barbecue Rub

Makes almost 2 cups

Ingredients:

- 1/2 cup sweet paprika
- 1/4 cup granulated sugar
- 2 tablespoons light brown sugar
- 2 tablespoons kosher salt
- 2 tablespoons freshly ground black pepper
- 2 tablespoons chili powder
- 2 tablespoons ground cumin
- 2 tablespoons granulated garlic
- 1 tablespoon dry mustard
- 2 teaspoons cayenne pepper

Method:

1. Combine all the ingredients and store in an airtight container in a cool, dry place. Will keep indefinitely.

Tomato Sauce

Makes 3½ cups

Ingredients:

- 1 tablespoon extra-virgin olive oil
- 2 garlic cloves, finely chopped
- 1 (28-ounce) can crushed tomatoes
- 10 fresh basil leaves
- Kosher salt
- Freshly ground black pepper

Method:

1. Bring the grill to 350°F with the cooking grate and heat deflector installed, then preheat a 5-quart cast iron Dutch oven on the grate with the grill lid closed.
2. Pour the oil into the Dutch oven and close the grill lid. Once hot, add the garlic. Close the grill lid and cook for 30 to 60 seconds or until the garlic is golden brown.
3. Add the tomatoes. Close the grill lid and cook, stirring once, until slightly thickened, about 20 minutes.
4. Remove the Dutch oven from the heat. Tear the basil leaves into the sauce. Season with salt and pepper.
5. Use immediately, or let cool and transfer to an airtight container. Refrigerate for up to 1 week.

Texas Brisket Rub

Makes about 1½ cups

Ingredients:

- 1/2 cup kosher salt
- 1/2 cup granulated garlic
- 1/3 cup freshly ground black pepper
- 1/4 cup sweet paprika (optional)

Method:

1. Combine all the ingredients and store in an airtight container in a cool, dry place.

Alabama White Barbecue Sauce

Makes about 1½ cups

Ingredients:

- 1 cup aioli
- 1/4 cup apple cider vinegar
- 1 jalapeño pepper, stemmed, seeded, and minced
- 1 teaspoon kosher salt
- 1 teaspoon cayenne pepper

Method:

1. In a small bowl, whisk together the aioli, vinegar, jalapeño, salt, and cayenne.
2. Transfer to an airtight container and refrigerate for up to 5 days.

Mojo Marinade

Makes 2 cups

Ingredients:

- 10 garlic cloves, smashed
- 1 tablespoon dried oregano
- 1 cup extra-virgin olive oil
- 1/2 cup freshly squeezed orange juice
- Juice of 1½ limes
- Juice of 1/2 lemon
- 1 tablespoon kosher salt
- Stems of 1 bunch fresh cilantro

Method:

1. In a medium saucepan, heat the garlic and oregano in the oil over medium heat for 1 to 2 minutes or until fragrant.
2. Turn off the heat, let cool, and add the orange juice, lime juice, lemon juice, salt, and cilantro stems. Transfer to the bowl of a small food processor. Blend until the cilantro stems are finely chopped. Transfer to an airtight container.
3. Refrigerate until completely chilled before using and up to 1 week.

Chimichurri

Makes 1/3 cup

Ingredients:

- 1 garlic clove, peeled
- 4 cups fresh flat-leaf parsley leaves (from about 4 bunches)
- Juice of 2 lemons
- 1/4 cup extra-virgin olive oil
- 1/2 teaspoon kosher salt
- 1/4 teaspoon cayenne pepper

Method:

1. Put the garlic, parsley, lemon juice, oil, salt, and cayenne in the bowl of a small food processor. Blend until emulsified and the parsley is finely chopped.
2. Transfer to an airtight container and refrigerate for up to 3 days.

Roasted Red Pepper Spread

Makes about 1/2 cup

Ingredients:

- 1 cup jarred roasted red peppers, drained
- 1 tablespoon extra-virgin olive oil
- 2 tablespoons freshly squeezed lemon juice
- 1/2 teaspoon cayenne pepper

Method:

1. Put the peppers, oil, lemon juice, and cayenne in the bowl of a small food processor. Blend until smooth.
2. Transfer to an airtight container, and refrigerate for up to 1 week.

Conclusion

Using one of these great products may seem daunting, but with the information in this book you will be cooking great food on your Kamado Smoker and Grill in no time. Get a copy of the Kamado Smoker and Grill Cookbook today and find out the most innovative and exciting recipes for delicious barbecue food!

Get a copy of this Kamado Smoker and Grill Cookbook today and find the most innovative and exciting recipes for delicious barbecue food!

Printed in the USA
CPSIA information can be obtained
at www.ICGtesting.com
LVHW081236271023
762324LV00008B/130

9 781639 350933